THE LAST CAMELOT
US Navy's "Secret City"

By J.C. Martin
Edited by Ian Conrardy

DORRANCE
PUBLISHING CO
EST. 1920
PITTSBURGH, PENNSYLVANIA 15238

The contents of this work, including, but not limited to, the accuracy of events, people, and places depicted; opinions expressed; permission to use previously published materials included; and any advice given or actions advocated are solely the responsibility of the author, who assumes all liability for said work and indemnifies the publisher against any claims stemming from publication of the work.

Dorrance Publishing Co
585 Alpha Drive
Suite 103
Pittsburgh, PA 15238
Visit our website at *www.dorrancebookstore.com*

ISBN: 978-1-6366-1495-3
eISBN: 978-1-6366-1674-2

Table of Contents

Prologue

I've thought many times over the years, especially now as I turn the corner into my seventies, how life takes me further from those days of yesteryear, the days of my youth. Many thoughts and memories that are driven by the nostalgic sounds of the fifties and sixties music, which, still today, I have push-buttoned on my car's satellite radio along with my country/western stations. It's said that "Hearing old music you used to love is like getting in touch with old friends."

The constant reminiscing I find myself doing with the same friends, family members, and many others from those long-ago days that still feel like yesterday brings about so many wonderful thoughts and memories, not only of our personal lives but also the sameplaces, events, and ventures we all experienced in the time we grew up there. We were together from our adolescent years, as teenagers, through four years of high school. It was a span of roughly twenty years, around 1950 through 1970. My time was 1953 through 1966. My memory doesn't clearly recall those great days before 1953 as I was only about five years old.

I laugh when I say my memory gets somewhat better through the late fifties and into the sixties, through my senior year at the only high school in the Indian Wells Valley of California. I'm laughing again as I'm reminded of what us Baby Boomers often say, "If you remember the sixties, you weren't there," obviously referring to the drugs, free love, and the party culture of the youth in that era. Let's see how well this ole memory does as I take us back in time. It's a time for me where adventures and events are still clear as if they happened yesterday. Yeah, that shouldn't be a problem! However, I'm relying mostly on memory so bear with me if I make some mistakes when it comes to details here or there.

The more difficult yet fun task will be describing the overall lifestyle during this special period from the perspective of those who grew up living in this "Camelot." It was most likely their first home and first way of life. This book is about those first kids in the place we all simply referred to as "The Base." However, it was more commonly known as The Naval Ordnance Test Station, China Lake, California.

This was a time in American history that I wouldn't hesitate to call "The New America." This was just several years after American dreams of home and family had to be put on hold as evil burned its way across the world. This great generation of patriotic Americans were forced to defend the American dream. Their American ways were being threatened by tyranny around the globe.

These post-war no-nonsense heroes, young and war-weary men and women became so anxious to get their lives back into swing and achieve that American dream with unbelievable desire. I'm sure there was a very "special gleam" for their love in the eyes of these war-weary husbands that, I won't hesitate to say, were the beginning of the baby boomer era. I state that with a huge smirk!

The American dream designed for family and friends to share with their children, to install them with integrity, honesty, god, country, and the American way. It's what they fought and, sadly, many died for. I'm sure that dream is exactly what started their journey that ended in this desert area of California at this brand-new Navy base called China Lake.

These first China Lakers, the young parents of that great generation, came together by the thousands from all parts of the country without knowing what in the hell to expect. They all came in hopes of the same thing; a permanent position working for the Navy and its mission at this new base in the desert. These young, post-war dreamers, unknown to each other at the time, each bringing an unbelievable enthusiasm with them, together built and developed an incredible community infrastructure for their families, friends, and the Navy's mission the likes of which one could have only dreamed.

Now it's been some seventy years since those far past memories for we who grew-up there, and the first kids of this new hidden oasis in the upper desert of California which we called the "Base." Those memories still seem like yesterday for those who lived there and experienced the lifestyle as it developed through the mid-forties and into the fifties and sixties. A special time in America when life was so much simpler for kids and, I assume, that this was typical of youth throughout the cities and towns of this country.

However, I do wonder how tight-knit other communities around the country really were, because we who lived there on Base at China Lake, isolated from the rest of the world, have always felt very special with regards to our unique community and with such pride, as if it had been built just for us kids by our parents. I'm curious if other kids of the same age across the country during that time period could say anything close about their community compared to the way we felt about our community on Base.

It was a community full of adventure, sports, faith, and educational facilities with a great school system. Designed to have an elementary school located in most housing territories, making school walking distance from home, easy for kids to attend a variety of different elementary schools, kindergarten through sixth grade. Attending so many different schools was, without a doubt, the biggest factor in these kid's ability to bond and develop so many different friendships and relationships. They got to know not just the kids from their own neighborhood but so many others of different ages through the variety of schools they attended on Base. Hundreds of these close friendships, if not best friendships, from those early days continue to this day so many years later.

Call me crazy for making such a big deal out of this, but I really think it's unique that so many, from so long ago, are still friends some sixty to seventy years later! So unique and interesting, it makes me kind of curious to compare kids from other town's or city communities throughout the country from that same time frame. Whereas, I'm sure most likely, a few of them became lifelong friends as they went through all their school years, from kindergarten through twelfth grade together. Yeah, no doubt there were a few but I'd be interested in how many of those kids, outside the China Lake Base, stay in touch with each other still today. Do they still stay in touch? Do they go on trips, golf, fish or hunt still together, some seventy years later? Hmm, maybe a few but nothing in comparison to the hundreds if not thousands of friendships of the kids from our home and way of life on Base at China Lake in the fifties and sixties, friendships that go on still today! This comparison, that difference I hope to illustrate throughout these writings,what my family and I experienced, growing up as an original part of the family of desert kids that lived the "Base" life in Post War America, us first kids of China Lake.

One other aspect to add to my theory is that of a well-balanced family: Two responsible and caring parents with well and encouraging discipline. I have to believe after the war this was the attitude and belief of the majority of Americans. On Base at China Lake the typical family I knew had both parents, the man who went every day to work and the mother stayed home. The priority of this teamwork was to have a home full of love and happiness but parented with a firm hand. To respect one another, other adults, and all fellow human beings. A secure, confident up-bringing, built with a lot of self-esteem.

Victor Hugo said, "The supreme happiness of life, is the conviction that we are loved." OR, as Sigmund Freud declared, "Love is the first requirement for mental health." I believe all of this contributes to a wonderful childhood with plenty of confidence and the capability to form multiple relationships at a young age, anywhere and anytime. We sure had this feeling growing up back in those days on Base.

Introduction

From the words of Edwin B. Hooper, vice admiral, U.S. Navy (retired) director of naval history in his introduction to the book: *Sailors, Scientists, and Rockets. History of the Naval Weapons Center, China Lake, California * Volume I*:

"The history of the Naval Ordnance Test Station developed from infancy to maturity over a period of twenty-four years is a story approaching miraculous. It is a story of the evolution of a concept, and from this concept, the creation and growth of a research and development complex unique in its scope and versatility. It is a story of individuals of great ability, imagination, determination and ingenuity; a story of inspiring leadership and remarkable teamwork involving naval officers and civilians of varied experiences and expertise."

The best way to introduce my childhood story to those who did not personally experience the same up-bringing, believe me there are thousands who actually did, as you will learn, is to start with a quick introduction by those brilliant naval minds responsible for the whole concept of bringing to life an infrastructure for those folks and their families. They came from all parts of the country in support of this massive military endeavor.

I have taken an excerpt from this great book in an effort to describe and illustrate this huge achievement, even to the point of highly underestimating the infrastructure that would eventually be required. Here in this excerpt titled "Community" is where my life along with so many thousands of others began.

"Original planning for the station, done mainly in Washington, Pasadena and San Diego, gave scant attention to the need of building a total community in the desert as an integral and necessary part of the station. Future years would show that the development of living conditions attractive to a high-caliber civilian staff was essential to the success of the Station's technical programs.

It was a foregone conclusion in the planning of the new station that the Navy would have to develop the needed housing and other community resources for its military personnel and civilian employees. The two existing communities in Indian Wells Valley, Inyokern and Ridgecrest, were both small desert villages with virtually no capability to meet a large and sudden demand for housing and commercial services. In planning a Navy-built community, the November planners considerably underestimated the size in relation to what it ultimately became. Their estimates were made when financial support probably would have been forthcoming for more housing and community services if requested. The report stated, "An estimated ultimate population of about 1,000 was used in prescribing the layout of the community." By comparison a decade later there would be 10,000 persons in the Navy community of China Lake and an additional 5,000 in the adjacent community of Ridgecrest.

Recognition that it should be a military-civilian community was reflected in the list of planned facilities, for example, commissary store (to be available to civilians) recreation facilities (to be available to civilians). Once Captain Burroughs and his staff were stationed at the site and experienced what "raw desert" really meant, they began to push forcefully for community development. At an informal meeting New Year's Day of 1944, Bureau of Yards and Docks and Bureau of Ordnance officers discussed the subjects of "The Village" and "Quarters for Civilians." They recognized that development of "The Village" was of "prime importance." And it was suggested that station housing be constructed independently of the National Housing Agency if possible, because, "It was believed that the type of houses being built under N.H.A. sponsorship would not be adequate for permanent quarters for the types of occupants which the Navy would be employing at a highly specialized research and test station." There was concern in any event that the National Housing Agency was not in a position at that time to finance the structures. There was fear that the assembling of substantiating data would delay the project. A subsequent check proved these concerns valid; the housing agency doubted whether it could approve funds for better housing than the "standard temporary minimum war housing unit." The dilemma was heightened by an earlier decision by the judge advocate general to the effect that Navy Appropriation Act funds were clearly not available for civilian housing. This was the initial setting for what would be a continuous concern of the station to make available living quarters and community services that would attract technical personnel of the level needed, except for the inclusion of civilian dormitories, no clue that this was the beginning of what would become the largest military-civilian community built and operated by the Navy.

Burroughs, in his facilities proposal made just prior to official establishment of the station, listed only four permanent living quarters in addition to the bachelor officers' quarters and barracks. These were for the commanding officer, head of training activities, head of experimental activities, and head of research activities. The Pasadena Planning Committee increased the list to include married officers' quarters for the commanding officer, executive officer, ten senior officers, and twenty junior officers, 100 low-cost housing units in addition to the bachelor officers' quarters, barracks, women's dormitory for 100 civilian women, and men's dormitory for 100 civilian men in nonprofessional grades. The November planners had foreseen a community of 1,000, but by February 1944, Burroughs estimated the Station's wartime population would exceed 2,000 people, a significant raising of the sights that were still far too low. He also estimated that during the eighteen-month construction period the civilian employees of contractors to be serviced by the Inyokern Post Office would number "perhaps two thousand." Burroughs' population estimates were made in his effort, which was successful, to keep the official post office address of the Station as U.S. Naval Ordnance Test Station, Inyokern, California, rather than have it changed to that desired by the postal authorities, namely, "The Naval Ordnance Test Station, Mojave, California." Such a change would have made it a part of the postal system of the town of Mojave over sixty miles away. Thus Inyokern, a hamlet of twenty-five people in 1943, became the name by which the station would become known the world over in the years immediately ahead. The fact that Burroughs underestimated the population by a factor of six indicates that not even he foresaw the full proportions of the station—or the extent of the development he would lead in the hectic days ahead.

CHAPTER 1

CAMELOT

Here in April of the year 2020, smack dab in the middle of a deadly pandemic, COVID-19 is keeping humanity boarded up in what is a recommended, but voluntary, quarantine. The quarantine is the best method along with social distancing, a new term to Americans vocabulary, in fighting this invisible enemy. Since I plan on staying home a lot more for the foreseeable future due to this virus, I figured what a great time to try something I've always thought someone, not exactly me for Christ's sake, with a decent talent for writing from the Baby Boomer generation who experienced the fifties and sixties growing up on Base at China Lake. Someone with the ability to put all those thoughts, memories, and stories that continue onto today into writing.

This may take a while so make a toddy, sit down and relax in a nice comfortable chair, and let me take us back in time. We're going back to those wonderful years of the fifties and sixties from the perspective of these first kids of China Lake. We'll look at their childhood through their teenage years growing up in that incredible community, that oasis in the upper desert of California.

It is so important for me to emphasize the importance of that great generation of parents, folks from all walks of life, who just a few years earlier engaged in a world war. It was a fight for survival for their beloved country and the dreams they sought. The American dream of marriage, family, and working hard at their jobs to support dreams of their own, dreams for their children to experience and benefit from.

American veterans just returning from war in the Pacific or the European theater, back home along with their families or just starting their families, all had one thing in common; they were looking for a steady, well-paying, and long-term employment to get their lives back on track. It amazes me how that "fortune of fate" for these young kids, these new "desert rats," came from our greatest generation, their parents. The parent's, unbeknownst to each other, came together to begin that new life. I'm sure none of them had any idea of what their future may bring, but they were likely surprised how quickly this dream became reality.

That influx of great, American civilians alongside military personal started around 1943 in the Mojave Desert just below the lower High Sierra mountain range in what is called the Indian Wells Valley. Across the country the US Navy had been advertising for a massive work force made up of the most intelligent minds (scientists and engineers) along with facilities support power and construction workers (electricians, plumbers, carpenters, laborers, painters, etc.). This great workforce, headed up by Navy command and supported by the Marine Corps, was established for the sole purpose of standing up a new base for testing and evaluation of the Navy's air & land arsenal. The area was approximately 1.1 million sq. acres (the size of Rhode Island) of land in a remote area of the Mojave Desert. In the Indian Wells Valley at Inyokern and, eventually, 8 miles east at the outskirts of the town of Ridgecrest the Naval Ordinance Test Station (N.O.T.S) at China Lake was born.

("In the views above the desolation of this site can be easily seen. There was to be a whole city and industrial complex to spring up out in the middle of nowhere. This was a very large undertaking, but it was needed. It has proven to be a very well planned and executed undertaking.")

NOWHERE IN PARTICULAR

Okay, so I had a great childhood, big deal. More often than not, a lot of people can say the same thing that they had an enjoyable upbringing with family and friends. Much more unique, my childhood wasn't from your normal place that has existed for some hundreds of years such as a city, a suburb or a town. No, it was on a special military base, established and stood-up just after the war in the Pacific. Developed in a huge area of desert, dirt floor. This mighty-million-acre military establishment called the Naval Ordinance Test Station (N.O.T.S) China Lake was brought to life in the early nineteen-forties for a new special Navy mission. Included in this massive military endeavor was a very small part of this million-acre base, maybe a ten square mile section, cut out for a whole new infrastructure for family living. It was designed and built for the men and women who worked on this special base but, much more specifically, for the children and young adults of these working parents, civilian and military alike. This was my first home, my first way of life, and, along with my family members and first ever friends, where my childhood began, unlike the many wonderful and great books written in the past about our beloved China Lake, about its beginning, the Navy's mission, the weaponry, and the famous names who had either lived there or toured there in support of the Navy. No, my intent is to describe China Lake in a little more of a fun way, from a new perspective, something different from those brilliant minds that have written so many books about this special place. My perspective will be a unique view about the base, from the eyes of the youth that lived there. I'm not talking about a few neighborhood kids, of which so many have their commonly told childhood stories. Stories about their city or town and maybe the few long-lost friends, jokes of their personal childhood ventures. No, I'm talking of a community of thousands of which so many hundreds of them, in their own age group and time frame over a span of twenty-five years, are still lifelong friends. To be able to describe in full detail the craziness, the ventures, and many special events experienced by all these youth, including the "First of the First" children, would be difficult. Simpler would be to describe how I personally experienced much of the common adventures, events, and activities that was experienced by all the kids at different times through that span of years on base at China Lake.

Our war weary patriotic parents, civilians and military alike, together brought to life what was nothing more than a desert landscape to form this community. It wasn't a town, nor a city but for us who lived here, what we called "The Base" or in military lingo "The Station."

A hard pan desert floor with masses of desert creosote (greasewood) bushes, tumbleweeds, and miserable winds was turned into an unbelievable utopia with an infrastructure designed with military precision for fun and play for us kids and our families. Unbeknownst to these new young tyrants of the desert, a historical and world-renowned Navy test and evaluation center was evolving to the likes of which the military world had never seen. It was developed in support of the Navy's mission, a community of beautifully designed homes and infrastructure all designed to support us who supported the Navy. Two and a half decades of growing up in a time of peace and security is hard to imagine, but for us, that's exactly the way it was.

That contingency of our greatest generation, of mostly war veterans, who together worked hand in hand to bring their kids a life that still to this day some 70 years later is referred to as what I like to call "Camelot." It was our mythical castled city in the desert or as some others call it, "The Secret City." Either way, I call it Camelot and I suppose it would be pertinent to explain why.

I'll always remember in the early days of 1960, during the inauguration of our country's thirty-fifth president, John F Kennedy, how patriotic and at peace people across the nation seemed. I especially recall the youth across the country and how we all felt so secure as we watched by way of television. We as kids were very new to politics and now we had the first family brought into our living room, watching rather than reading about this young and new Catholic president and his beautiful family that represented us so well as a country. It was perhaps the closest to an American royal family there had ever been.

To my memory, and I'm sure I can speak for most kids during this time in history, it was the first time we really thought about life in the White House and the first family that occupied it. This was also the time when I first heard the term "Camelot" and learned its significance to the first family. It meant, "A time, place, or atmosphere of idyllic peace, justice, and happiness." As Romance writer and Arthurian scholar Norris J. Lacy commented that, "Camelot, located nowhere in particular, can be anywhere." That was exactly how we felt at that time in our young lives, peace and happiness, doing our best to be friends with everyone!

I use the term Camelot to describe in one word how we felt and lived our lives in the late fifties and early sixties. I hope I'm speaking for the rest of the folks that grew up with me on the base at that time. Although, I imagine living and growing up on a military base installed much more patriotism than usual in us all. It certainly felt good, safe and secure.

Unfortunately, that beautiful way of life we were experiencing didn't last much longer. Our happy little lives came to a halt when 1,036 days later something horrible happened. In Dallas, Texas for a Trade Mart luncheon, President Kennedy's procession left the airport and traveled a ten-mile route that wound through downtown Dallas in front of an excited, cheering crowd. The President's motorcade turned-off Main Street at the Dealey Plaza around 12:30 P.M. and was passing the Texas School Depository on that unforgettable, November 22, 1963 day. Moments later, an assassin's bullet ended our nations beautiful and idyllic atmosphere.

Now an Eternal Flame at the John F Kennedy's presidential memorial at our thirty-fifth president's gravesite in Arlington National Cemetery in Virginia is all that's left. The flame and our memories to remember those wonderful days of "Camelot." It was one of the biggest tragedies in American history and we witnessed it from our TV sets at home on base at China Lake. Like many others, I'll never forget where I was that unforgettable morning.

A LITTLE CONTEXT

For you folks reading the story of this historic military installation and have never experienced the Navy's China Lake base but may have read or heard about it through books, stories, or even TV, it's important to understand how quickly it was built and actually became the first home and way of life for thousands of children. It began in the mid-forties, on into the fifties and early sixties through their graduation from high school and beyond. This mythical "Secret City" on this base in the desert came to life and was enjoyed by so many children, teenagers, and adults alike during different times in the span of some twenty-five years. Then, just like in a good mystery story, this wonderful "Family Oasis" in the middle of the desert of California, just as quick as it was built, had disappeared, vanished in the night. Gone!

All those houses that held so many fun desert life stories, kid adventures, and wonderful events. All the schools and the stories within them, all gone like the zebra-tail lizard, far quicker than they were first built.

Now for those who had the opportunity to experience that special desert life, all that they have left is their personal stories when they so often got together on fishing or hunting trips, parties, dinner, or just over a beer. This is the case for so many lifelong friends who all grew-up on Base, no matter which time frame, in that span of some twenty-five years. Nothing to cry over, no way! Life goes on, to laugh at all the stories with the folks that experienced that same ole way of life together. The same as we have over the past half century and as we still do today and will continue to do until we are no longer here to do so!

My story is for those folks to add another chapter of reminiscing about their childhood and wonderful years, to bring back old memories of that special life you may have forgotten but now brought back to life, dusted off from the halls of the memory to enjoy once again. I do hope others will enjoy and find as interesting as all us who experienced that wonderful time.

I think it's so important to emphasize again as I re-visit in the coming chapters so many friends' parents, coaches, and so many supporting adults that were so involved in the eyes of us kids bringing our community to the closes point to utopia as could be. We never asked, and they really never talked about it, but every one of these great folks from that greatest generation one way or the other came from just several years earlier fighting for their life, family and country. I won't be discussing much or writing about these hero's heroic ventures during their service in the defense of our country, nor would they want me to. I will say that I do know the hell many of these war veterans did go through and the sacrifice's they endeared.

Let me just say this: These great folks loved their base as much as their children did. To know still today, that from a life they provided so many happy, fun stories and tales of those days at China Lake by their children who grew-up there are still visited and enjoyed, so often by so many still today. How we all so enjoyed our life, as we know they also did, would be reward enough to these great Americans.

I still shed happy tears, I still raise my beer to cheer when together with so many others from those wonderful years, to these great Americans who selfishly provided us with such a wonderful, happy childhood. Our own Camelot...

MY BEGINNING

I can only speak from a limited perspective about my family's journey west to California from the mountains of Huntington, West Virginia. Knowing my dad, as I had over the following sixty years, I can only imagine how he convinced his young wife and mother of four boys of this great opportunity and long-term career for civil engineers in a beautiful desert oasis of California. "Yes honey. California!" They likely read over it many times with many discussions of this dream opportunity opening out west.

Basically, the US Navy's national advertising effort for, not only Dad's field, civil engineers with construction backgrounds, but for chemists, scientists, physicists, and all types of engineers and construction workers along with the infrastructure support of public works (DPW) from the likes of plumbers, electricians, carpenters, and maintenance technicians. All these roles were for the obvious support required when starting an endeavor of such a huge magnitude which the Navy had never embarked. Thousands of new homes and community support facilities, including beautiful sports fields, parks and swimming pools, and stores and shops, all capable of supporting an influx of personal and their families as they came to work for the Navy and its mission.

The Navy's mission is so well documented and found in the halls of the U.S. military and Navy history in so many books and stories that have been written that I have no need to add too, at least from the military perspective. No, my version is to be different and unique from the perspective of the Navy. My focus is the people, civilians, military, and their families, who helped build this amazing community.

My family, in early 1949, was made up of mom (Mary), dad (Charlie), my oldest brother David, my second oldest brother Steve, the one and only third oldest son Roger (my mischievous future mentor in crime) and of course me, the 8-month-old baby. Mom often told the story that I took my first steps at 8 months old in the spring of 1949, as we stopped for a rest and lunch at the Great Salt Lakes of Utah on our way to Dad's new job and our new home in California. I can almost picture this venture, as with so many other times in future family trips or outings.

I remember mom would layout several blankets that she had clearly carried with her for such occasions, to lay her babies down for naps while she brought out all the ingredients to make lunch for her wary chauffer (dad) and her "Precious Angels." As Mom continued her story, she would say she had looked up from her motherly duties only to see her 8-month-old baby boy, standing up for his first time and heading to the Great Salt Lake! The first steps in my life were taken while on my way to my new desert home in the great state of California. I can still picture Pop saying, "Yeah, alright, a gamer," while watching his little tyrant take his first steps. With a chuckle I can also picture my two older brothers, each with their hands over their mouths laughing and not alerting mom to their little brother heading down to that beach of salt!

Over the years I still remember so many stories besides the ones told by my parents. These were mostly from the mothers of my friends and of their first reaction when seeing California's "Oasis in the Desert." It's a beautiful location in the Indian Wells Valley called China Lake, "seriously thinking there was actually a fucking lake," as they came in droves to start their new life. A life in their new Navy-provided home and to raise their families, at least for the foreseeable future. My mother's version is so typical of the stories from most others, including the ones I heard second hand.

I just wonder how many of these folks didn't stay, who this may have included? I get a good laugh at some of their hearsay comments after first sight of the base. They flipped their cars around with boat in tow and headed back to wherever they had come. As I understood there were quite a few. My mom's story, which I've heard many times, has never strayed.

She says it was on a spring afternoon. I can picture coming down from Little Lake on the back roads from Utah, heading south toward Inyokern on the old two lane 395, just passing the cut off road to Nine Mile Canyon maybe eight miles north of Inyokern. (What's kind of funny about this statement is I have no idea why I picture us coming the northern back way down from Little Lake since I don't believe Mom ever said what direction we came! It's just how I imagined or pictured it, but hell, it may have indeed been that exact way. Oh well, whatever.)

She described her anxiety while looking east down over the valley prepa-
ring for her first bird's eye view of her new home in California's beautiful
"Oasis in the Desert." Unfortunately for her that's not quite an apt description!
She would continue, "The dust and wind were blowing so hard," it was her
first welcoming sight through the blowing dust and of the indigenous creosote
bushes. "I began crying!" she said, "the only thing Charles (dad) could say was,
well, you better get used to it because we don't have the money to turn
around." My poor mother, this god-sent devoted catholic, this Saint Mary and
her "Joseph the Carpenter" and four little lambs, straight out of the mountains
of Huntington, West Virginia after leaving behind the only home she ever
knew. Her devoted parents, six sisters, and brother were all devout Catholics.
I'm positive she could never have imagined what this new venture in this hot
California desert would become. Her daily prayers and belief in god absolutely
guided her light.

(The new Mrs. Charles C. Martin)

I was too young to remember the days of our family's arrival to China Lake, (N.O.T.S.). I know that our first house was located on McIntire in what I believe the Navy referred to as a Normac. It was a duplex style house with a high front porch and steps down to a small front yard with a few new young trees trying to stay alive. The McIntire house was located a few blocks north where the All-Faith chapel sits now, just across the main thoroughfare and the center of all base activity, the Bennington Plaza. I'm not sure how long we lived on McIntire, but it couldn't have been more than a year or two.

It must be hard for one to imagine as I speak of it today. This was a massive construction undertaking, part of the Navy's mission. The Navy was developing large support facilities at an enormous rate in and around this desert-mountain base of some 1.1 million square acres of ranges and desert flat ground. It was ideal for the Navy's testing of aircraft, missiles, and rockets. Major facilities such as the airfield support buildings of so many different size including aircraft hangers, runways, world renowned laboratories, and so many other support buildings in and around the base ranges. This massive construction endeavor was the responsibility of the office of the Officer in Charge of

Construction which was headed up by the Navy's career construction officers and their civilian counter parts. The civilians were a part of the construction office of civil engineer experts and inspectors, including the one and only civil engineer, Charlie Martin, my dad.

(Charlie in his Navy SEABEE'S uniform) Dad as a young dapper civil engineer

CHAPTER 2
Center Of Activity

All that activity also included the continued construction of the housing and its support facilities. Again, I'm speaking around the late 1940's and into the turn of the decade, the 1950's, as the base housing continued growing as support families poured onto the base. As the housing units were built and brought on line, they became the responsibility of the newly formed Housing Department, managed by the first Housing Department head, Mr. Cal Fallgatter. Actually, I'm really not sure if he was the first department head, but he was the first housing manager that I remember! He was a very personable and well-liked guy of the first families on base and had one of the larger families. I think my Dad, Charlie, and Cal had a competition going, or maybe it was the two wives Ginny and my mom, Mary! One of Cal's sons, John, and I went through the school system together, being the same age and graduates of the local and only high school in the valley, Burroughs and the Class of 66.

Mr. Fallgatter organized and totally controlled new base family housing placements. This massive housing community was developed around the main centralized center of activity, which ran west to east from the main front gate of the base and up and down Blandy Avenue, the main thoroughfare. Many of these support businesses in the center of activity were recreational and the responsibility of the Special Services Division of the base and who designed and ran all the Navy's sports programs.

(Blandy Avenue)

I can't exactly say I knew who the Special Services position titles held by these folks back in the early days, but I believe my dad's good friend, Chuck Mangle, was involved with Special Services. He was a big help in getting Hollywood stars and pro baseball guys from Southern California to the base for special events such as Little League's Opening Night. I also think Chuck wrote a column in the sports section of the base newspaper, The Rocketeer, and was also an associate pro scout for the Cincinnati Reds. Other memorable special service guys I remember were, Ray Guyer, John Shroff, and later Marty Denkin.

The center of activity, that huge plaza-like facility, connected many support facilities such as the Navy Exchange, commissary, base theater, gymnasium, and the large indoor pool. Additionally, it contained small supporting shops such as the base barber shop where most guys got their hair cut. The barber shop was managed, at least in the very early years, by Ray Eastman and Joe Perry, two large and older black men, who cut hair for many years including my brother's and mine. That was the case until my dad decided to be our barber. I'm sure it was to save money with all the hair needing cut. Our problem was he only had one way of cutting hair, "Cut off the sides and leave some on the top." Real fucking cool, five brothers with the same shitty, hillbilly looking hairdo. Not cool! Although, I laugh when thinking about it today!

Sorry, I got a bit off track. I'm sure it won't be the last time as I reminisce. Anyway, another small shop located in the plaza was the cobbler shop and shoe repair. It was owned by the Navy and managed by a large, well-liked personable gentleman that everyone knew as "Corny." His real name was Bob Cornelius. Steve Metcalf liked to joke about when getting new shoes, saying that Corny's balls would always stare out at him as Corny sat on his little stool fitting Metcalf's shoes on him. Geez, I mean, as many times Corny fitted me with shoes, I just can't say I would be watching his balls! Only "The Dogman," Steve's nickname, would notice that shit.

Some other spots on the plaza were the library and pharmacy. All these support facilities, stores, and shops were connected by a ten-foot-wide concrete walkway roofed with a Kelly-green painted wood roof with the same green V support posts about thirty feet apart from one end to the other. This was a massive shopping center, approximately three blocks long, called the Bennington Plaza. It was named after the Navy's small carrier during WWII, the USS Bennington.

(Looking S/E from the parking lot at the Commissary and Navy Exchange)

(Looking west at Bennington Plaza. Blandy Avenue far right. The movie theater and Gym, Top of center.)

(Looking S/E at the Commissary and PX center and Library far left from the parking lot)

Although, I do have to admit, I for one nor anyone I ran with ever called it Bennington Plaza. Geez, I'm not even sure as kids we knew the frickin' name? We'd just say, "We're going to the gym, the movies, the show, or the Exchange." I don't remember anyone say, "We're going to the Bennington Plaza."

The Special Services Department also managed and maintained all other recreation facilities on base, including the different types of ballfields around the main shopping center and the many parks throughout the housing communities. As the Special Services grew into the late sixties, they continued to offer new recreational activity ideas or items to the base folks. One of these new programs was the renting of outdoor camping and boating equipment for the outdoor enthusiasts.

The Sierra Nevada mountain range is, by far, the most beautiful area of lakes and mountains in the western states and just hours away from our home on the Base. Charlie really wasn't much of an outdoor, mountain type guy, so my family didn't get up to these beautiful areas too much as kids. However, we made up for it once we grew older and were living off base. Many of my friends did grow up visiting these lakes and hunting in the mountains, starting at a young age living on base. I still today go fishing and hunting with many of them up in the local and higher range of mountains, guys like Gordy Irvin, Albert Hyles, of course Herbie Pinto, Metcalf, and Tom Chapman to name a few. Chapman, who also grew up on "the Base" with us, is considered an expert of the Sierra Nevada mountain ranges and has written several books on the subject. His Pop also was one of the main guys that helped the building of desert and mountain guzzlers which were, basically, man-made watering holes for game birds such as quail and Chukar, both of which are indigenous to the high desert and mountainous areas of the Base and surrounding territory.

As I reminisce, I can remember Gordy, Herbie, and I hunting Chukar up on top of Black Mountain Peak, just south, maybe twenty miles from the Base. As we were heading down a steep, very narrow ravine, Gordy and I were practically shoulder to shoulder with me on the right side, when a covey of Chukar flushed up in front of us. We both swung up our shotguns and at the same time to blast a round. Suddenly we hear Gordy holler out loud as he grabbed his ear! Well, the problem was, I'm left-handed and as I raised my shotgun up to my left side right next to Gordy's ear. Oh shit! To this day Gordy has ringing in his ear. Well, at least he says he does! Let me just say, Gordy has repaid me ten times over for that mishap. That was just one of hundreds of stories we have just from hunting and fishing with so many different friends over the years. Anyway, I've gotten off the beaten path a bit by going into "after living on Base," but we do have so many stories from that time.

BASE HOUSING

It was a time where it seems everyone was treated with respect, especially our parents and all adults. It was a time when us kids spent most of our summer days outside in the desert, riding our bikes, at the ball fields, or playing pick-up games in the alleys or streets. I remember when picking teams for sports (skins vs. shirts), I always tried to be skins because I was always uncomfortable getting sweaty in a shirt. I just didn't like playing with my shirt on!

A typical Sandlot baseball pick-up game always began by choosing teams with the kids that were there to play that protector day, usually consisting of at least ten if not more guys, including the Rowe Street Gang! Once captains were chosen, usually the two best players then they would pick their teams.

It was a time when you could stay away from home, at least until the sun went down, then we just needed to be in hollering distance of our parents in case they were looking for us.

During the summer evenings, if we weren't at a little league game or another planned activity, we'd be out around the neighborhood, again in parents' hollering distance, playing some kind of game with other neighborhood kids. Games like Hide & Seek, Ditch-em, or just sitting around bullshitting about kid stuff until the streetlights would come on, which was the sign for all kids to head home for the night.

It was a time when sitting at the dinner table in the summer maybe happened only several times a week, for sure on Sundays due to the verity of summer activity of all the kids in our family. Much different than in the winter time when, as a family, we always had dinner early and together every night, including grace before dinner so homework, if not completed, could get done and the dishes were done by whoever's turn it was amongst us kids. We had never heard of a dishwasher back in those days, it was all done by hands by us kids!

Another thing that was so memorable that we liked to do many times in the summer months as we got older, say around 8 or 9, was sleeping outside in the yard, mostly my two brothers, Roger and Duke and me, but many times with the Rowe Street Gang friends, like Jimmy Nichols, Bobby and Mike Sorge, either at our house or theirs! Yep, just throw a blanket on the grass with a pillow and sheet or a sleeping bag. We'd just grab-ass around and tell stories under the billions of stars, no worries in the world.

We slept outside a lot in those younger days, as it was just so much cooler than inside the warmer house and also much quieter, very peaceful and easy to fall asleep too. Now I must be honest as we got a little older and continued sleeping outside, we didn't exactly hang around our yards bullshitting that much. No, we became a little more adventurous as we started roaming the neighborhood or other territories late at night, not really getting into mischief. Hmm, maybe I better rephrase that, not causing harm to other's or their property. Ha Ha. What we liked doing is harassing the base security that cruised the streets at night in their Navy gray trucks!

Again, keep in mind we knew these neighborhoods like the back of our hand, I mean the alleys, tree ditches, and all the places we knew the base police trucks couldn't go or get through. Why? Well, it was just a real rush for all of us, when we'd see a Base police truck coming down the road, say 2 A.M. as we would run across the street maybe a half mile in front of them, just far enough to give us a head start. Oh yeah, they'd come after us, that's for sure, but for all the times we played our little game with the "Night Shift," as we called them, we never once got caught. I mean we'd just haul ass and head into the alleys or tree ditches or even into one of the small desert areas that were in some of the territories. There was always bushes, hedges, or trees to hide behind and we knew what and where those trucks could or couldn't go! Just a real rush, that's all it was. Another type of ditch-em!

This large housing community, as us kids came to know so very well, was split up in several sections, depending on where one worked and what one did for the base, basically the "pecking order" starting with the higher-ranking military personal and their highest-ranking civilian counterparts according to an established Government Service (GS) rating system. The highest (say GS-16) of the civil service pay rate such as the scientists and physicist on down to the middle ranking engineers (GS-9's and up) and on down to the public works and service workers (GS-5's +). The most prestigious of housing was in an area just east of the Center Plaza and up the hill to what became known as "The Hill" community or "Snob Hill" as it was called if you didn't live there, where a real Navy jet aircraft welcomed you to the notorious Officers Club ("O Club").

(A great aerial view looking down at the Plaza (bottom right) with Blandy Avenue running east up the hill to the Officers club (just left of the Plaza) and the new SOQ's behind the "O" Club and of course the "dry" Mirror Lake left (south) of the SOQ's.)

That beautiful facility included large banquet rooms, bars, along with dining and dancing areas inside. As you go outside in the back of the large main building was the huge canopied stage surrounded by a very large dining and dancing area, made just for "under the desert stars" dining, dancing, and entertainment called the Lani, all surrounded by beautifully manicured hedges and lush green grass with several walkways leading up to the large outside swimming pool. Sitting on about ten acres, this Navy landmark facility was basically your main entrance to the "Hill" community and approximately 200 Senior Officers Quarters (SSQ), the largest of the housing units on base. Made up of pink brick and stucco duplexes and single units of three, four, and five bedrooms, many if not all with wood, parquet type floors, even some of the biggest units had fireplaces! "Fireplaces," un-heard of elsewhere on base.

These SSQ quarters were later declared by the Navy to be considered historical, and along with the Officers Club, still stand at China Lake today and are documented as historical Navy facilities.

I would guess as just an estimate from what I've heard over the years, there was approximately 2,500 housing units on base at its peak. I'm sure this would have to include the 500 Capehart units. 250 of which were called Capehart A and built up on the Hill, just north of the SOQ's, close to the base golf course.

The first 250 Capehart B's were built at the far south end of the Base housing in a large area of undeveloped desert, which at the time was the Rowe Street Gangs main lizard hunting territory located between the housing units on Rowe St, where my family lived at 58 A Rowe and the newly constructed Burroughs High School. An area of maybe 500 acres about a mile south through the desert and then directly west all the way to Vieweg School. The two Capehart housing developments, consisting of new, navy wide state of the art housing of three and four bedroom single units were built and brought on line in the early sixties as the first base housing grew older, and the need for newer housing for personal and their families were needed. These two Capehart housing communities became a big part of our lives; as for me and all my friends who have been on base most of our lives, these houses came on line during our 5th/6th grade time frame, through junior high and early high school years, say 1958 to 1963.

In the late forties and early fifties, most likely around the same time or just after the SOQ's were built on "Snob Hill," the majority of base housing was finished or being completed in several different areas around the base and made up of a few different styles of housing. The first of these housing units that were built from ground-up were, as I believe the Navy referred to them, Normac housing. These were all duplexes of two and three bedroom type of wood construction and plaster type siding. This housing section was located some ten to fifteen blocks deep just north of the Plaza and Blandy Avenue and heading west to the Navy hospital, "Dispensary." This small group of housing, approximately 100 or so were the only houses north of the Plaza. The balance of housing was referred to by the Navy as Hawthorns, Prefab's, and Duplexes, built of concrete construction of flat roof, two and three bedroom duplex units maybe averaging 1400 sq. ft. of interior. The Prefabs were replaced in 1963 as the Capehart's came on line.

Just a note: Above I mentioned "built from ground up" I say this because, from my understanding, the Navy, in the very early days, actually found some old Army type barracks buildings that the city of Bishop, California, about 100 miles north up the road from China Lake, used for, from what I understand, housed troops during the war. Needing housing quick the Navy brought these unoccupied barracks down to the Base and converted them into separate living quarters. They named these type of housing "The Bishops" and housed the earliest of the work force. Once the new construction of housing was built, these Bishops, I assume, were removed or used for warehousing and storage.

The navy's Prefab's and Duplex housing were located from south-east of the main plaza continuing south for several miles, paralleling Richmond road, the back-gate road of the base, which fronts the west side of Mirror Lake to where the base Dump land fill begins. Yep, a lake! Well, not quite, but we'll get into that a bit later. Anyway, these types of housing, which, again, I believe the Navy referred to as Duplex's and Prefab's, continued from its most southern point then due west to its furthest point at Vieweg Elementary School at the far west end of Rowe Street. This total section of housing consisted of some 1,300 housing homes. This section of housing and it's streets, back alleys, and tree ditches alone with a few large desert areas was basically the majority of our gangs stomping grounds, until about the time I hit 8th grade and my parents moved our family up to the new Capehart A housing up on the hill. Oh god, not a "Snob Hill guy." There goes the neighborhood! Ha Ha.

There also was the Navy's Wherry housing community just outside the back gate and a mile west. It was located maybe two or three miles directly south across the desert from my house on Rowe street. That was at least until the new Burroughs High School was built between my house and the two hundred or so Wherry houses, which I will assume sat on Navy land. I really didn't know much about these houses at the time but did became friends with many who lived in them that I knew from on-base schools and activities. Besides some single officer quarters, dorms, and some small U-shape apartment complexes and many one bedroom with a shower and shitter for single folks working for the base, these were basically the several communities of housing areas on base, all located in this area that may have seemed small to adults but was huge to us little kids. It was the main center for living, shopping, and recreation, just this small tiny piece maybe 10 miles square of land aboard this massive military complex, the Navy Ordnance Test Station, (N.O.T.S) at China Lake. This small, centralized portion of this massive complex was where brilliant minds came together with engineers, a large contingency of service workers, and their military counterparts, away from the daily and in some place's dangerous activity, supporting the huge Navy endeavor on this enormous land mass to raise their families in this small infrastructure. It was designed not just for these parents' entertainment but mainly for the huge contingency of kids of all ages growing up on Base.

In a nutshell, these were the first several thousand civilian and military families; the first families to stand-up this new city on this Navy base. Their kids were brought here early in their lives or were born on base or maybe later in Ridgecrest. They all lived and grew up together in this small community located in the middle of this brand-new naval base of historical portions. These great American veterans went to their duty stations or work by day in each supporting effort for the mission of the US Navy and the fleet, of which us kids, especially at a younger age, had not a clue what our Pop's did for or in support of the Navy and its mission. Yet, as we continued growing, we all felt and grew to know the importance and the pride that we had from what we saw and heard every day of our lives. A lot of that mainly came from the aircraft that flew daily over our heads, what we referred to as "The Sound of Freedom."

However, nights and weekends were all about the kids and this was done by utilizing the entertainment structure that these parents planned, designed, and built for this mass influx of young, adolescent and teenage kids over those first few years. They did it with their own sweat and time with huge support from the Contracts Division and Public Works department. Utilizing its heavy-duty equipment, they built state of the art playfields, facilities, and programs for this mass influx of young first kids of China Lake.

(The first phase of housing development at China Lake is complete in April 1948. Located in the distant South portion of NOTS are the Prefabs, Hawthorns and Duplexes. The Prefabs were gone by Summer 1963. The New Duplexes weren't completed for another four years. Left to Right Center is the Officers Club, Bank, Library, Commissary, Navy X, Theater, Enlisted Men's club and Station Pool. Burroughs High was located one block South. Good shade trees were a few years away.)

(Development was fairly complete at NOTS by 1964 with the new Burroughs High School adjacent to Wherry Housing (top L), the New Duplexes and the All Faith Chapel (lower center). Ridgecrest and China Lake Blvd. and the Midway can be located the distance. A noticeable increase in cars and parking lots can be found.)

CHAPTER 3
The Rowe Street Gang

As I mentioned earlier, we first lived on McIntire St. followed by a quick stop south across the base on Rodman Street, which included my parents fifth son, my younger brother Richard Alan, aka "Duke," as my oldest brother David eventually nicknamed him, as Dave did for all his siblings. This was around the time I changed my birth name. Instead of Christopher John, I wanted to be called John Christopher or just John. As I recall I had to beat up some smart-ass kid for calling me Chrissy-Missy and I felt I had a girl's name, so from that day on I wanted to change my name, no big deal!

Anyways, my dad got an opportunity for another three-bedroom house on Rowe street with much more outside yard, which included the front, one side, and back, located the next street over east from Rodman and about half way south between Langley Street and Vieweg Elementary School. At this time, I'm four or maybe five years old and my family is moving into our home for many years to come at 58-A Rowe.

Similar to our house on 58-A Rowe

Family photo on Rowe Street

This was the house where the rest of the Charlie and Mary Martin's clan came into the picture starting with the younger, but oldest, daughter, Marion. Next the sixth and seventh sons, Paul and Drew. Finally, the last of the clan, two more sisters, Ann and Liz. In 1958 we lost sister Ann, a two-year-old little beauty, in a terrible car accident on Rowe street. It was a pretty devastating time for us all in the Charlie & Mary Martin family.

Note of interest: A year or two after my sister, Ann's, passing the Catholic Diocese in Fresno, California, funded and ordered a new church be built in Ridgecrest. This new facility was named St. Ann's Catholic Church. Included with the new church, a very tall statue of the Holy Mother, St. Ann, with her hand on the shoulder of a young child to sit high above the entrance to this new church. The French artist, needing a picture or photo of a young little girl to design the child's face for his sculpture, was provided a photo of my sister Ann to use for the young saint's face! Still to this day, she looks over the good folks of the Ridgecrest and China Lake area as they enter this house of worship.

With so many kids, although several hadn't even arrived at this time, in this small three-bedroom, two bath Navy home, Charlie and Mom came up with an idea to alleviate this problem. They bought and brought home, placing it in the side back yard, a 50-foot two-bedroom type trailer for the two oldest, Dave and Steve, to live. This certainly had to have relieved some of the problem my parents had for sleeping arrangements for sure, but to be honest, I really can't remember the sleeping situation that we even had. I do remember

Roger, Duke, and I were always in the same room together, but that's about it. This big trailer worked out pretty nice for the Rowe Street Gang when the two oldest brothers moved out most of the year for college, unbeknownst to Dave and Steve leaving us a perfect place for our poker games and a fort to just hang out and grab-ass!

I remember back at 58-A Rowe us kids would occasionally pull some tricks on our parents, all in family fun, that usually would include one of our parents. For example, one time my Dad was working on the financial books for the Knights of Columbus, a Catholic church support group, for which my Dad was the secretary treasurer. As he worked on his monthly financial report, with all the books scattered around on his desk, we all waited patiently for Pop to get up and use the bathroom. Finally, the time came. While he was out of the room, we made our move by placing a large, twelve inch in diameter fake puke on top of his books and then placed the family cat up on the desk to make it look as if the cat puked on his books!

We all, including Mom, hustled back to watching TV with one eye on Pop as he came back into the room. As he got ready to sit back down, he spotted the fake puke and right away threw his pen into the stack of books as he started cussing, grabbing the cat, and tossing him off the books and across the room. I really don't have many memories of Dad cussing much so this was relatively new for him and all of us when he verbally stated, well, "Shit-fire-hell." I mean, call the priest will ya'! He was obviously pissed while all us were in the room, seemingly oblivious to the situation; he turned to look at us all on the couch, trying to hold are laughter. W e just couldn't anymore and we all burst out laughing. Then he knew he'd been duped as he picked up the fake puck and tossed it at us with a big, somewhat embarrassing smile on his face!

According to my memory, life as a young China Lake "desert rat" basically began here on Rowe St. and just as with any new place my brothers and I quickly began to adapt. Just behind our house was a large alley and of course our Navy gray dumpster along with three rolls of large Salt Peter trees watered and maintained weekly by the base public works. We called the person who tended those trees their "Tree Ditch Man." In his Navy gray Jeep, he would drive very slowly on the tree ditch road located between the first and second tree rolls.

I bring up the tree ditch man to illustrate how mischievous us young, desert tyrants, "Mom's little Angels," had started to become. We would dam up the water flow serving the tree rolls for our own little swimming hole, of course the biggest fun would be after our swim breaking the huge dam we built, only to flood the whole damn area! More of our mischief and I'm sure more irritable to our tree ditch man was the little traps we'd lay for him such as digging a three-foot-deep, two-foot-wide trench covered with branches and weeds across his tree ditch road. Never did get caught for that trap nor did we ever witness the Jeep going into the trench. It was funny at the time, hope the poor guy didn't get hurt; as I mentioned, he slowly drove the tree ditch road.

These three rolls of trees started north at Langley St., past Rowe School and followed Rowe St. all the way up its south side, maybe 2 or 3 miles, to Vieweg School. Just on the other side of the tree ditches was all desert which you could see for several miles towards the town of Ridgecrest. The importance of these tree ditches to us was their use as our hang out and all the cool forts we would build. When I say "our," I'm talking about us middle three brothers, Roger, Duke, and myself. Dave and Steve were five and seven years older and had their own buddies. They weren't about to hang with "The Rat Men" as David so graciously nicknamed us and our friends.

I clearly remember and laugh thinking about how Dave's high school buddies thought the "Rat Men" name for his little brothers was just funny as shit. There was Sammy Gregory and Tommy George, two of the funniest and well liked of Dave's friends. Also, there was Lowell Dietz and Rich Cashore, who were cool guys which I liked a lot. They just loved calling us "Rat Men" for fun!

Roger, Duke, and I became friends with many of the kids on base. Most were either from school, church, baseball, or the many other activities the base had to offer. Our closest friends during these times on Rowe street were the kids living on or around Rowe Street. It was basically our territory.

Back down Rowe Street toward Langley and just across from Rowe Street School, another elementary school made from Navy metal Quonset huts, lived the Sorge family. Made up of four boys and three younger sisters, Christen, Karen, and Marta. The oldest two boys, Wally and Denny, were my brother's Dave and Steve's age and then Bobby, a year older than Roger and Michael (Da' Dikes as was his nick name), who was my age, and both were part of our group or gang that ran together. Unfortunately, in the summer of 1960 just after graduating from high school we lost the older brother Wally to some ulcer problem. As young kids we really didn't understand the circumstances, but we do remember Mr. and Mrs. Sorge were not happy with the Drummond hospital.

Down the street from the Sorge's on Langley were the Mead brothers. The oldest was Richard, a year older than Bobby Sorge. Next was Mike who was a year younger than me and the youngest of the brothers, Pat, maybe two years younger than his brother Mike.

Just behind the Sorge house across their back ally to Rodman, everyone on base it seemed had a back ally and a gray dumpster, was Jimmy Nicol's house, the closest at that time to Roger and me. Jimmy was the only boy in his family with two much older sisters. His parents, Pete and Polly, were well known not only from their contributions in support of the community, but also, they owned and distributed the weekly Green Sheet, later renamed "The Swap Sheet." It was a kind of local news bulletin and community affairs list. It also served as a lost & found. It was a gauge sale swap meet style green sheet and advertisement for folks around the valley. In addition to mowing lawns, pushing and loading groceries in cars for ladies coming out of the commissary, or selling lemonade or cool aide to make some money at a young age, we also stapled the thousands of pages of the Swap Sheet each week for Jimmy's parents.

Also, across the street from Nicol's on Rodman was a large family of mainly girls named the Coffee's. As I recall, Paula Coffee was Bobby's age and the others were a few years older than me. I believe they all went to St. Ann's Catholic School in Ridgecrest until high school. There was also another family of girls, the Nelligan's. The ones that I knew, Sue, who was Roger's age, and Nancy, who was a few years younger than me. They lived a few doors north of the Coffee's on Rodman. I have to admit, these two families certainly prettied up the neighborhood!

Next door to the Sorge's on the northside lived the McGlothlin's. Mr. and Mrs. McGlothlin, Jack and Isabell, who were probably my parent's best friends, had four boys of their own. The oldest, John, was my brother Dave's age and close friends with him. Bob was the second oldest. He was my brother Steve's age. Mike was our age and was also in our gang. Finally, there was their little brother Joe, who was young, maybe three or four. The older brothers, John and Bob, were good friends with my older brothers and the Sorge's oldest brothers, Wally and Denny.

Unfortunately, Mr. McGlothlin (Jack) who was a huge supporter, member, and president of the little league program on Base, had an apparent heart attack at a young age, I believe in his forties, and passed away. It was devastating to the whole community and so sad for our buddy, Mike, losing his Pop. Shortly after his passing, Mrs. McGlothlin moved her boys back to her hometown in the Washington, D.C. area. The new little league field just finished during Jack's little league presidency was memorialized in Jack's name "Jack McGlothlin Field." They were some special folks!

Just across the street from my house and two houses down were the Pecks. Mr. and Mrs. Peck were close friends with Mel and Doris Sorge. They had three daughters. I can't remember the name of the oldest. The middle daughter, Evelyn, who was Rogers age, and the youngest, Charlette, a couple years younger than me and who I'm still friends with today. They also had a son Jimmy, who was my age and also ran with the Rowe Street Gang.

To this day I still can't explain why Jimmy (Peck) was more picked on by our gang, especially by the older guys. Maybe it was since he got pissed off so easily and got all red and huffy to go with his flaming red hair. It just didn't make a pretty sight and he was quite easy to agitate. He seemed to get into a lot of fights!

I remember one time we had a deep underground fort in our backyard and my Mom made us close it up and bury the hole. Of course, because we were good little angels, most of the gang was burying the hole with dirt and lots of water. Well, it turns out we kind of made ourselves some quicksand some five or six feet deep in this large hole. Obviously, we needed to test the quicksand for its, let's just say, consistency. Sure! Well, Bobby and Roger snuck over behind Peck and without notice pushed him in. Peck started cussing and screaming at Bobby and Roger as he slowly started sinking. We all stood around laughing hysterically as we watched Peck slowly going under. We started to worry a little as he slowly sunk so we hustled around looking for a branch, board, or something of enough strength and length to throw out to Jimmy. A forethought we overlooked as usual with our spontaneous jokes.

Finally, I found a strong tree limb and quickly got it to Jimmy's only hand that was visible along with his nose and popping scared looking eyes and flaming red hair. As he grabbed the branch, we were able to pull his scared ass over to shore and out of the quicksand. Afterwards, as he slowly came back to normal and his red face back to calm from being pissed and scared. Now he was simply happy to be alive! Yep, it was a close call that we all laughed about later, including Peck! Oh yes, mischievous, "Moms Little Angels!"

Another fort story that I'm really not to proud speaking about ended up involving my poor mom, the last person we'd ever dream of getting hurt by our fuck ups! We had a great fort in the back yard which was mainly underground tunnels with several different rooms. Keep in mind back in those days we didn't have a clothes dryer, so Mom always hung the laundry up on the four-string, wire clothesline with clothes pins, which hid are little back yard secrets from the kitchen window, and believe me, she had a lot of laundry to dry. A white, clean smelling barrier between good & mischievous.

We had a mattress in one of these rooms which was lit up with candles so we could look at our "nudie" magazines and smoke cigarettes. Yeah, we were ten maybe eleven years old, a little young for smoking and reading nudie books, but the whole gang did. Well, one morning a lot of us were in the fort. I can't remember exactly who, I'm sure besides me and Roger, most likely Nickols and Bobby Sorge. We somehow caught the mattress on fire, and it started smoking like shit. We scrambled to try and put it out, but it got so smokey that we had to get out. Well, my mom was doing dishes in the kitchen saw the smoke pouring out of the cave and ran out to help as we started pulling the burning mattress out of the fort. When we finally got it removed and put out the fire, we were all standing there talking about the near miss when my Mom showed us her hands. She had blisters on her fingers and under her nails from the fire! We all felt pretty bad about that! It was the last fort we ever made in our back yard. Father Ryan wasn't too happy in confession that next Saturday. Oh Lord!

58-A Rowe was also just a cross the street to Mr. Joe Stone's family's house. Many folks on base knew Mr. Stone from his archery range which he had built just outside his side yard, in the little alleyway between his house and the house next door to him. He also included a huge hobby shop for all the accessories needed for archery. I do remember in the late fifties, the China Lake Archery club had their own place located just southeast of the base dump, south across the Pilot Plant Road almost to East Ridgecrest Blvd. This was on maybe an acre of land with a large Quonset hut as a club house and several archery ranges with circle targets attached to hay bales for target shooting. I'm not sure why

Mr. Stone had this archery range at his house. Even more, how the Base allowed him to do so. Oh well, the Base let him, and he did it, end of story!

Mr. Stone's range was cool to have across the street as a few of my brothers, including me, were over at Stone's quite a bit. Although, I must add, Mr. Stone had several good looking daughters. Harriett and her older sister Phillis, both around Roger's age. Our brother Steve, who was always at Stone's archery range with his buddy Brain Cowan, became exceptionally good, maybe even experts in archery, and the two traveled together to many state and national tournaments and other promotional events. Kind of like, in a different way, my older brother David who, for some ungodly reason, got very good with a Yo-Yo, that's right, a frickin' Yo-Yo! He could do some of the most unbelievable tricks with that damn thing, not just one, but two at a time. He was in county and state tournaments in Yo-Yoing!

Standing Left to Right: Brother Steve, Brian Cowan, and Tom Ward Kneeling Left to Right: Terry Houge, (?), Brother Roger

Anyways, back at Stone's, one-night Roger and I were across the street at the archery range shooting some arrows as one other guy, Lyle Freedman, a fat mouthy kid back when he was younger, was working on his shooting. Mr. Stone was in his house having dinner while Roger and I were screwing around a little, like trying to stick the long sharp metal quivers, used to stick in the ground to hold arrows, into Mr. Stones side fence. Roger broke his quiver, so we stashed it and finished our set of shooting. When Mr. Stone finally came back out, Lyle told him that we were throwing the quivers and we broke one. Mr. Stone got pissed at us and sent us home for the rest of the night. We were not happy with our little friend and decided we needed to have Freedman pay for his misdeed of being a squealer, a narc, a snitch. That was a no-no to the Martin boys! Freedman had to pay.

We knew right where he lived and exactly the path he would take home, down the back ally, about a block from Stone's house. Lyle, I believe, was the same age as me, around ten at the time and very heavy as was the rest of his family, at least at that time. I say that because Lyle and his whole family, a few years later apparently, went on some kind of diet or stomach stapling, whatever they did and all lost a remarkable amount of weight and, as I recall, kept it off! Actually, Lyle and I were pretty good friends through high school.

Anyways, Roger and I, dressed in long bath robes and mom's stockings over our heads, found Freeman in the back ally and gave him a little whooping. That all sounds pretty bad now doesn't it? Well, we only punched him a few times, nothing really serious, just to get our point across. Geez, by the way he started screaming you'd think we ripped his fucking head off. I mean he squealed like a butchered pig. "I know who you guys are!" we heard as we ran back up the ally. Yeah, no shit he did. By the time we got back home, some five minutes or so later, Mom was waiting for us and said she had just gotten off the phone with Mrs. Freedman. "She said you two beat up Lyle." Well, we couldn't get out of this one and it cost us a week of restriction! Oh yes, mischievous we were! We got our point across…

Another guy I remember with some distinction from the Rowe Street days was the Helms Bakery man in his yellow woody-type panel truck he'd drive around the base housing, usually in the evening, at least around our neighborhood. His truck had several levels of six-foot-long tray drawers behind double doors in the back of the truck that he would pull completely out to display so many different types of great looking donuts and cookies. The distinction I recall was that the bakery man looked so much like Clark Kent, glasses and all, you know, Superman.

Roger, Duke, and I would always be hanging around when the Bakery man showed up on Rowe Street with his strange whistle-type horn. He would pull over for us, as we looked like we wanted to buy something, which sometimes we did if Mom gave us some money. He did keep a good eye on us "Little Angels," which made it tough to get a couple freebies. I do remember a few times the three of us at the same time as we hung around his truck, and I'm sure "Clark" had no idea what mischief we were up too when, at the same time, we'd go, "And, who disguised as Clark Kent, a mild-mannered reporter from the Daily Planet," just having fun mocking our bakery man!

LIZARD HUNTING

The huge desert area on the other side of the tree ditch rolls, before the 250 Capehart-B housings and the new Burroughs High School were built, was our gang's main lizard and snake hunting territory. We'd get started very early on a lizard-hunting summer day, usually by Jimmy Nicol's, crossing the ally to the Sorge house while giving the "gang call," always with Bootsy his dog, a great lizard hunter and hole digger always out front leading the way on lizard hunts. I have to go off track a little again as my memory is recalling this one particular lizard hunt when Bootsy took off after a lizard that finally went into a bush. Boosey went right into the bush, nose first and came right back out yapping and howling. Yep, a Sidewinder trying to nap in the bush didn't take to kindly to this dog poking his nose around. Yep, right on the cheek this sidewinder bit Bootsy! It didn't take long for the dog to start getting a little sick as his cheek continued puffing up. Fortunately, dogs may get a little sick and swell up a bit as the venom works through their system, but after a few days, they will recover back to normal, which is exactly what the dog did! "That Bootsy was a real lizard hunt-in warrior," a loyal and true Rowe Street Gang member for many years!

Anyways, back to Nicol's giving the "gang call" as he'd headup Rowe street, picking up Bobby and Mike Sorge and their dog Rascal and then Peck on the way up to our house. Nicol's could do the call better than any of us, although we all did it fairly well. This was our gathering call for years and it came from deep down in our little boy's voice and sounded like an owl sound. Impossible to do as we got much older, it went like "Oh-oh-oh....oh-oh-oh-oh" and could be heard for blocks. You here that and you knew the Rowe St.

Gang was around! Ha-Ha-Ha, lots of fun.

Usually, from our house after filling our canteens with water from the hose, we'd head out into the desert and the morning cool air, knowing that once the sun got higher so did the temperature. We all, most of the time, wore jeans and tennis shoes. Converse, no doubt while in the desert, and t-shirts were more optional and if worn would usually come off sometime along the hunt for being too hot or used to help grab and hold on to a Leopard Lizard, Chuckwalla, or Red Raiser, all of which could bite fairly hard and certainly would draw blood. We also always carried nice long sticks, usually with a fork type end, perfect for the sidewinders and rattlers. Yep, we hunted for them too, but they were hard to find, and when we did find them, they were usually sleeping or on their way to a new bush or spot of shade, and we'd just stumble into them. I've always said I really believe the rattlesnakes knew we were coming and hid from us! They didn't want anything to do with "the desert human tyrants."

I mean, we ruled the desert. Seriously, as we grew older, say ten to twelve years old, we, usually most of the Rowe St. gang, would do the "B" Mountain venture, the only mountain anywhere close to us and still located on the base. We'd of course start out early as we always did, especially with the long walk ahead of us as we'd head through the desert toward B Mountain, some ten miles or so from our house. We'd always do a quick stop at the Stables. It was a place just below the B on the mountain with maybe five fenced-in corrals for Base residents to board their horses. I believe this was offered through Special Service's for those few folks who actually owned horses. The stables also included a few shacks that also had water hookups to refill our water bottles before going on up the mountain.

Once on the mountain, we usually spent all day hunting, mainly Chuckwalla's. They liked basking in the sun on the hot rocks. Catching these varmints was a feat, when seeing us coming, they would run and hide in cracks of the rocks and blow themselves up with air, making them tightly secured and tougher than shit to get out! Oh my god could those pricks bite and they would not let go! We'd usually catch at least one every trip to bring home with us.

The ugly chuckwalla

We also had found, while up on the mountain, a few spots on our many trips that had sand domes that we could get up high above and, with a running start from about 30 feet above, jump and fly through the sky. It seemed like forever to us little kids and landing and tumbling some thirty feet down into the large area of built-up sand domes. For sure some of our most fun desert ventures for years were those "B" Mountain trips!

To this day, I still tell the desert story of when my brothers Steve, Roger, Duke, and I were lizard hunting one early Sunday morning, out fairly deep in the desert with a BB-gun, which was not allowed for the kids of the base, at least in the housing areas. When we spotted a Base gray pickup coming through the desert toward us some mile or two away. One of us yelled cops and Steve hauled ass through the desert to hide the BB gun and then ran back to us just as the cop drove up. Steve, breathing like a panting dog, Roger, and I down on one knee as if looking in a lizard hole, and fucking Duke standing there stiff as a board, like at attention, as if he was ready to shit in his pants. The cop looked at Steve and said, "What you guys doing?" "Lizard hunting sir," Steve answered. "That right?" looking at Roger and me. "Yes sir." Then he looks over at the statue and said to Duke, "How 'bout you?" Duke says, "We don't have a BB-gun, we don't have any BB's." No shit! There went our BB-gun! Ole Steve was so pissed at Duke after the cop made him go all the way back and get the gun. We laugh at that today! Just one of those funnier and memorable ventures in the desert I will always remember.

All the kids in the different neighborhoods had their weapons of choice. Sounds like gang wars, huh? Not at all, the weapons I'm taking about would be like slingshots or BB-Guns type weaponry, nothing more than to shoot lizards or aggressive dogs and shit like that. The Rowe Street Gang's weapon of choice was the blow dart gun. A piece of metal or steel hollow pipe, maybe three feet long. We would tear a half page out of a Look magazine and roll-it up into a pointed, ten-inch dart; if we wanted to make it even more lethal, we'd slip a needle or pin at the tip just before rolling the dart tightly then licking with spit the length of the dart to hold in place. Once fitted and tightly secured in the blow pipe it was ready to shoot or blow. I'm telling ya', this dart could be blown a good hundred yards. That's right, the length of a football field. Closely shot it certainly could do some damage, especially with the pin at the tip!

Booty and Rascal were our guinea pigs when testing our accuracy. In fairness we'd give them some distance or running start before practicing, but that really didn't last long because these dogs were too smart, and when they saw the blow guns come out, they wouldn't leave our side. I mean they stuck to us like stink-on-shit. I can't remember anyone getting seriously injured, at least nothing more than having a dart stuck in the back or in your ass from one of the guys screwing around, and of course, it was always reciprocated one way or another! Yep, only the Rowe Street Gang.

As young little rats living out in the desert most of our adolescent summer lives, and for sure not zoologists, or more specifically, herpetologists, we had our own names for every lizard that lived in the desert around the Base, not to say some names may be close to their scientific names, who knows? Like maybe, the Horn toad, that's the name we had. Anyway, starting from the smaller ones we had our desert names starting with "The Side-blotch," a small, dark, worthless lizard not worth chasing. "The Gecko," hard to find, usually under wood, an unusual, almost see-through lizard. The fastest little shit in the desert was the "Zebra-tail," desert sand in color with its beautiful rainbow sides, always a challenge to run down. "The Whip-tail," dark scaled with a long tail averaging maybe eight inches or so and the first of the pricks that would bite, although not very hard, wouldn't draw blood. "The Iguana or Crested," as we called it and the most likeable. These guys could grow much bigger than most; they were desert sand in color and averaged around 15 inches or so. The most popular to chase and catch, usually by digging them out from their hole, tail first. Also, what was very interesting about the Crested was many times we'd find several tails on these guys. Believe it or not the most tails on one Crested, I remember very well, was the one we caught that had five tails. No Shit! A rarity for sure.

Then there was the vicious "Leopard lizard," more of a rarity to find but could bite harder than any other desert lizards. For those two reasons we were always excited when running into a Leopard. It was a challenge! Then there were the scorpions, we never liked and usually killed them. Finally, of course, the friendly Tarantulas that were harmless, and after we let them climb around on our arms a while, we'd always let these guys go! Anyways, this was basically the China Lake desert lizard types that we chased all summer long in our young early days in our desert in the fifties.

CHAPTER 4
Street Territories

I know as I start reminiscing and visiting the past base housing territory's and the many kids who lived in each of these areas, especially some of my close friends and best friends of which I have no problem remembering, obviously, but I know I will certainly forget or miss so many more. I'm talking about thousands of kids, those first China Laker's. I can say with confidence, over roughly twenty years, the majority of these kids, one way or the other, directly knew or knew of each other during that time period of the fifties and sixties and beyond.

All the streets throughout the base housing communities, from all the kid's perspectives, were basically split up into territories. Those who lived on those streets, well, that was their territory. Our Rowe Street Gang's basic territory was maybe twenty blocks or so wide and included many streets beside just Rowe St. There was Rodman, Ringgold, and West Langley to name most of them. Like all the territories on base these kids, these first China Lakers, each in their own age group, became friends and grew up together through the years and on into high school and beyond. In my territory, I personally had close friends that one time or another I ran with, had the same school classes together, went to church, or maybe played baseball together, whatever the occasion. Kids like Jimmy Thomas who had an older brother, John, who was close to my brother Dave's age lived on Rodman. Gary Whitnack, Terry Hogue, and his older brother Danny who was Bobby Sorge's age and lived further up Rodman St. toward Vewieg School.

Reminiscing again as I start thinking of these guys. In this case I'm thinking of Jimmy and Terry! Jimmy Thomas and Terry Hogue in their younger years, say before eighth grade, lived just a few blocks from each other and were best of friends. I hung with these two guys quite a bit back then, and coming from experience, let me tell you these two guys were something else when together! I mean like a Laurel and Hardy team except they both were very large guys. Terry, even at 12 years old, you could tell he was going to be a big guy. Turns out he ended his high school years at around six foot four" and maybe 220 lb., no fat and I believe all league lineman at Burros football. On the other hand, there was Jimmy the other half of the duet, maybe 6 foot by eighth grade, a good-looking guy with dark, black Elvis like hair but very large and becoming more overweight as he grew.

Anyway, these two characters were best of friends, but Terry would get so agitated and was always harping on Jimmy and the two would argue constantly! I will never forget one summer morning they both came over to my house on Rowe Street to see the tunnel fort we had in the back yard. Roger and Terry went down into the tunnel and several of its rooms we had tunneled off from the fort's main room. Meanwhile, Thomas was outside in the yard bullshitting with me walking around outside the fort. Not paying attention where he was, walked on top of the thin roof of one of the rooms we'd tunneled. With Jimmy's weight all in one place on top of the fort, it all caved in, taking him with it. Well, it just happened to be exactly were Terry was sitting below in the fort when the roof all came crashing in!

Oh my gosh, I cry laughing still to this day, remembering how pissed Terry was at Jimmy. Jimmy scrambled to get out of this hole he created. Terry completely covered with dirt was trying to grab Jimmy as he screamed every cuss word in his vocabulary. Terry's problem was he was buried up past his waist and couldn't move anything but his arms, totally covered in dirt as he continued yelling, unable to grab Thomas. I'm standing there above the fort just crying, I was laughing so hard at these two knuckleheads. A true Laurel and Hardy moment for sure! By the way, we had to dig Hogue out of the hole! Oh, he was pissed…

Bruce Bell, who lived up the street by the Hogue's is another friend I remember well along with his younger brother Gary and their family. Bruce and I ran a lot together around fourth grade when we both attended Vieweg

School. Also a few people I knew, but not well, was Johnny Howell and his nice-looking sister Trudy who lived several doors down from us on Rowe, straight across the street from Peck. Down the street toward the Sorge's lived Gary Maxwell, my age, and someone I knew very well through many years at many of the same schools. He lived catty-corner to Jimmy Thomas on a short road that came off Rowe street, I think it was Smith street. Gary had the misfortune at a young age of contracting Polio, and I must say he has endured through the hardships all the years with such an admiring, positive attitude, and to this day, we are still friends.

Across this little street from the Maxwells, a couple doors up from the Sorge's, was Danny Miller. Several years younger from me, his gang of younger kids gave our Rowe Street Gang the utmost respect, similar to the respect we gave the Tomac Gang. Just across the shared back ally of the Meads on West Langley was Independence St. and then the next street over, Hornet Street, on the south side of Groves School, then Groves Street on the north side of the school. In this territory of some fifteen blocks or so lived some of my closest friends, mainly from school and sports. To this day we are still close friends.

Growing up on Independence was Teddy Sprouse and Bobby Brown and two streets over on Groves Street, just across from Groves School, lived Albert Hyles. Just up the street, Steve Troy, then further to the west of Groves, there lived Charlie Walker and his two-year older brother, Bobby, all five guys were my age. Besides going to school through the years together we also played little league and pony and colt league baseball against each other, as we were always on different teams, except for post season All Stars. This only lasted until high School when we all played together on the same high school team.

Across the street from Teddy on Independence close to Bobby was the notorious Karen Marker, a tough, good looking leader of the girl's movement of the fifties. Just kidding, but she was definitely well respected amongst her peers, especially the girls. She also happened to be my first actual girlfriend when we entered the third grade, even if she could pound me. Yep, third grade and still good friends today. Karen also had a gang of girls she ran with from in and around her neighborhood territory, her aunt and still best friend today, Barbara Roberts, Susan Jeffery's, Ellen Allen, Teddy's sister Gloria, and another toughie, Sissy Quinn (who was two years older than us). She also had an older brother, Billy, who, along with Karen's older brother Ronnie from this territory, were well liked and popular athletes. These two guys were amongst many of the older, quality athletes in the valley who we admired through their high school years in the late fifties and early sixties.

Sissie also had a younger brother our age, Robert, that also went through the school system with us. Directly east on Impendence and Hornet Streets across one of the main thoroughfares, Lauritsen Road and heading toward Mirror Lake was the neighborhood or territory of some more very close friends. We Rowe Street guys called this neighborhood the Tomac territory, said with much respect, especially when we were younger kids. We knew of Danny Tomac, several years older than us and one of the badass dudes on Base all the way through high school, along with his running buddies (gang) that he hung with, like Ted Friend or Teddy Bear, as most called him, Raymond Kelso, a well-liked all-around guy from the neighborhood pre-fab houses, and Tom Mather from the Wherry Housing community, who was best friends with Tomac throughout their lives!

I remember they had the coolest cave fort, dug into little hills of Caliche (Like harden clay) in the desert west of where Langley and Lorenzen road met, just across the little desert from Rowe Street school. Several of my good friends also lived in this same neighborhood, Gordy Irvin, Charlie Depew, and Herbie Pinto, a Navajo Indian and who's dad, Ralph, was a former Marine and notorious "Code Talker" during the war in the Pacific. Also, Eddie Lusher and up a street or two on Fowler Tom Chapman. Also, Ronnie Zills, a year older than me, was a great athlete at Burros and his younger sister, a year younger than me, Nita. These desert dawgs along with, as I mentioned, Albert, Bobby, and Teddy from back up the road a few miles on west Independence, including Karen Marker and all her gang of girl's plus, from the other side of Groves School, Steve Troy, Charlie Walker and another guy who I still see from our class, Daryl Silberberg, from this territory were all the same age group and first China Lakers that went through grade school, junior high, and high school together! The ones that are still alive, are all still friends today.

Also, a few of the better-looking girls on base came from this territory. Mainly, to just name a few, during my high school years I got to know Pasty Allen and younger sister Connie, two wild and crazy girls and very attractive in their teen years. Also, their cousin Ann Allen, who was my age and went through school with me. Also, her older and lovely Burros cheerleading sister and I'd say, just about "Miss Everything," Rita, who I got to know much later in life. I found her as beautiful inside as out. I also believe my good friends and also classmates throughout my school year life Jimmy, Lana, and Randy Kline, one-year older brother, a family of very talented singing voices that we enjoyed for many years, lived in this territory.

In another territory, just north of the Plaza, were the older houses, Normac, or whatever the Navy called them, where my family first lived on McIntire back in 1949. In these small, several blocks of houses lived some more close friends of mine who I also went through all the school years and sports together. Tom Kleine, Ernie Davidove, and Steve Oldfield all lived on or just off Mitchner street and very close to McIntire. Also, just a few blocks east on Wasp road, across the street and just west from Richmond school was another good friend Steve Metcalf and his highly respected family. Also, a few more well-known and respected China Lakers on Wasp Road were the Shull family, older brother Larry and younger sister Bev, our age, and a few houses over another popular and respected base family, the two lovely Riggs sisters, older sister Fran, and three years younger Cindy.

It is important to me that I highlight the special parents of these three families that lived on Wasp Road for years. Hal and Wonda Metcalf, Bud and Dot Shull, and Leroy and Ditty Riggs. I knew them all fairly well and all three of these first China Lake parents were all very involved with not only Navy activity but toward the support of their community, especially toward the teenagers of the base. They loved the kids and supported us all.

Except for Ernie, who was two years older, the rest of this territory's first China Lake kids I've mentioned, plus so many more our same age, all went through many different grade schools at different times and then junior high and into high school all together and still to this day are good friends. Unfortunately, we lost Ernie in the late sixties to the Vietnam War, one of the First China Laker and friend and sadly not the last that we lost to that crazy Asian war.

I always like telling the story about Ernie and his best friend, Gordy (Irvin). During a nice beautiful, fall Sunday morning I was just minding my own business while listening to some tunes on my parent's station wagon radio. Just coming from church going the normal 20-25 mph as I drove down Blandy

Av. right around "The Dez" (Station Restaurant). All of a sudden, my driver side door opened up and Gordy or Ernie grabbed my arm and both yelled "hey!" at me, scaring the living shit out of me, while they both sat riding on their well-known Honda 250 scrambler motorcycles. As everyone on base knew, for these two bandits, this was not an uncommon prank. That time really caught me off guard, to say the least. After I cleaned my shorts out, the three of us had a good laugh about it. Crazy shit for sure!

I haven't mentioned the two, A and B Capehart housing sites, on each side of the base that came online in the early to mid-sixties and much later than the housing that I was talking about earlier. I do remember when the construction on the Capehart B began and for several years, while my family still lived at 58-A Rowe, these houses were being built on the desert side of the tree ditches. One thing I remember during this period of time is that we, the Rowe Street Gang, maybe 10 to 12 years old or so at this time, made a small fortune from all the construction workers who came to this unbelievable hot desert (probably a hell hole, in their minds) to work on this Site B housing tract. We sold coke bottles filled with lemonade that we made from those five-cent frozen cans that made a gallon of lemonade. Like, we could fill 10 or so empty and clean coke bottles with real cold lemonade and sold them anywhere from $1.00 to $5.00 each, depending on what they had in their pockets and of course, for some reason, we never carried change. These sweaty, dehydrated construction workers just loved seeing these little desert humanoid kids coming with box loads of filled coke bottles of lemonade or Cool Aid (an even better return on our money).

On an occasion, we'd even make a bunch of peanut butter & jelly sandwiches around lunch time. They just loved those pb & j's. It's no wonder that all the Rowe street gang had plenty of money for our weekly, if not several times a week, poker games. Yep, ten, eleven, and twelve-year-old little angels with Poker games of twenty to thirty dollar pots! We all did well at Capehart B.

The Capehart A housing was the last of the houses built on the Base and were completed around my eighth-grade year, 1962, time frame. Located due north of the Officers Club, between the pink brick houses on Kearsarge St and the China Lake golf course to the north, approximately two blocks wide. With Richmond school to the far west and Blueridge Street at the far east end.

It was a two-mile-long and a quarter mile-wide housing territory of new state-of-the-art housing, maybe three miles or so from B Mountain. All the streets in this territory were named after Navy warships and carriers protecting America in the Pacific during WWII.

There were two main roads from west to east, Kearsarge and Ticonderoga with four streets, Midway, Leyte, Intrepid, and Blueridge connecting these two main streets and then three inter circles or half circles as they come in and out of Ticonderoga. They were Bogue, Shangri-La, and Coral Sea circles. My family moved to the hill Capehart's around my eighth-grade year, around the 1961-62 timeframe and we lived at 214 Shangri-La Circle, and yeah, no duplex! A new and spacious house for our very large family, even with Dave and Steve out and gone to college, we still had seven of us plus the parents living here. Yep, still needed bunk beds! More than just the house we had a great, and I have to say, crazy neighborhood. With that comment I should just add the whole damn, crazy Capehart A territory! Let me explain what I mean!

Starting from the far west, Midway street next to Richmond school, but also including all those kids on the other side of Richmond school that I have already mentioned that lived on Wasp road, Steve, and Mark Metcalf, the Shulls and Riggs. Back over west on Midway was Janis Little, another of the kids we all went through school together with and who I must admit, besides being a pretty gal, like her Mom, was always involved in every club, event, or activity there was, especially throughout our high school years. I mean Ms. Participation! The next street east was Coral Sea Circle where Big Gary Whitnack and his parents moved after living back in our old territory on Rodman. Across the street from Whitnack was a new kid on the scene in 1965, a Navy kid and great linebacker at Burros, Mike Kinne, (nick-named Kinna) who became very close to Roger, me, and our family. I'll never forget one winter evening after dinner, Roger and I were over at Gary Whitnack's and shooting pool with Gary, Kinna, and Buddy Phillips, another friend from Ridgecrest. All being seniors, except for me, and top varsity football players at the time. We were in Whitnack's spare bedroom turned into a poolroom with screenless, open windows looking outside to the street. Buddy and Whitnack, both with hardcore, bottomless pits (stomachs), got into a friendly argument over who could eat the worst shit. Gary goes into his pantry and brings back two open cans of Skippy dog food. Buddy takes his can and starts shoveling dog food out into his mouth with his fingers until the can was empty, saying, "Is this all you can come up with?" Then Gary, in a more polite way, dished his dog food out into a bowl and began eating until he was finished. I mean like it was some kind of dessert! Well, excuse me and my week-ass stomach but my head was out the open window throwing up my dinner I had a few hours earlier…you can believe it, if you knew these two goofballs, trust me!

On Ticonderoga, just where it intersects with Leyte, were some first China Lakers, the De 'Santo family. Jimmy (AKA Nut Man) was my brother Roger's age and his younger sister Sally, around our age, a real cutie who was Bobby Brown's girlfriend in high school. Also, Sally's younger sister Mary and much younger brother Mike. The next circle over, Shangri-La, was an unbelievable street of neighbors. When we moved there the Sorge's had already been there maybe six months or so and again, just down the street from us on the corner of Ticonderoga and the east exit out of Shangri-La Circle. Next door to Dikes was the beautiful Vicki Romero, a year younger than me, who's dad was the brother of the famous movie star Cesar Romero. Directly across the street from Vicki was the emphases Paul Sampson, a Special Service manager and golf pro at the base golf course. Just a great older guy and friends with the youth of the base.

Not done yet, next door on the east side of our house were the Livingston family with two boys a little younger but good guys, Bruce and John. Our house sat at the top of Shangri-La Circle with a sidewalk leading through the back ally that came out on Kearsarge Street, just in front of Jack Perce's house and who I road to school with in his hot 57' Chevy my junior year at Burroughs. I believe Jacks dad, Harold, was at some point Superintendent of schools. A couple houses west in the Capehart side of Kearsarge lived Stan Shafler, and just a few houses up (east) from Jack's was the Grant Penny family. Mr. Penny, always involved in the school systems, eventually became superintendent of schools. I believe just after Mr. Perce and was highly respected and a well-known family of the Base.

There were three sisters, Diane, Pam (who I knew and was in her wedding with Mike Kinne), and younger sister Kathy. Also, two sons, the older, Bob, and youngest son, John, from Burros Class of 60, maybe a year younger than my brother Dave. He was also a great athlete out of high school. Pretty much a hero and mentor to all us young athletes coming up behind him who followed sports in the Indian Wells Valley. Unfortunately, and so devastating to the family and the community, we lost John to the Vietnam war in the late sixties! Such a tough time for Grant and his family.

Anyway, where was I? Oh yeah, on the other side of the walkway from my house was our west side neighbors, Lt. Commander Howard Rutledge and his lovely wife and family. His oldest and cute daughter Sondra, who I was friends with and kind of a big brother to. I do remember one time during her eighth-grade year, my freshmen year, this pretty lass learned how to French kiss by her sweet, experienced, mom's little angel, neighbor! Hey, she asked me to teach her!

So much has already been written about that patriotic family and without a doubt had sacrificed more for our country than any family I have personally ever known. Commander Rutledge's seven-year imprisonment along with Senator John McCain and many other POW heroes at the enemies "Hanoi Hilton" prison in Vietnam, the unfortunate accident to his oldest son, Johnny, his unsuccessful run for Senate upon his return home from captivity, and his book "In the Eyes of My Enemy," all of which is well documented in US Navy and American history. What isn't documented and if I may bring a little humor from a much earlier and happier time in the life of this great family.

It just so happened that the Rutledge family, Sorge family, and our family were all on the same party line, typical in the early days on Base, common phone line's shared by two or three neighbors. So this one night my brother (guess who?), yep, Roger, was on the phone with his girlfriend Dee when the Commander interrupted the call, announced who he was and that he was the duty officer of the day and had to make an emergency call! So fuckin' Roger pop's off with something like, "I don't care who you are, I'm here first and visiting with my friend." Oh, Lordy a definite military no-no. I mean within minutes the commander was at our front door with my dad, and did he let this civilian know that he was not happy with his son's rude phone manners and so on and so forth with his admonishment! I think my dad may have got a little of his own ass back as he took ALL Roger's ass that night.

Anyways, moving east to Bogue Circle and Blueridge where I had more friends, mainly military family kids. Also, my mom's sister, Betty, who followed my mom out west from West Virginia looking for employment, met and married her China Lake husband LeRoy Doig, a very highly respected physicist she had met while working on Base in the early fifties. They along with their 4 children, my cousins of which the oldest, Lee, who was born on the base, is considered today an expert on the subject of China Lake, lived at the corner of Kearsarge and Blueridge Street, where, on every Thanksgiving, the two families met for Thanksgiving dinner.

Also close to my Aunt Betty's house on Blueridge was James "Pokey" Bowman and his older brother Rick. Pokey and I ran together, I mean like brothers, for several years in high school during his Dad's tour at China Lake. A few other military families I was friends with during their dad's tours at the Base were the Hughes sisters, older sister Betty, Rogers class and a year younger, and sister Karen who I speak more about later as Ms. Little League. Back over on Blueridge lived a good friend of the Hughes sisters, Leanne Lippincott, and her older brother and a great athlete, Link, who I played Burros baseball with before their dads three-year tour of duty was finished and they moved on. Link did go on and play football for Joe Paterno at Penn State.

So growing up on the "Hill" in the site A Capehart neighborhood as teenagers, this bunch of mis-fit kids, most on Base since childhood and going through pony and colt league baseball and four years of all the high school sports together. All popular Burroughs athletes, where, from the eyes of the general public, not only the Base but the Indian Wells Valley community were just typical mischievous teenagers, all-around pillars of the community, an inspiration to the youth of the future. On the surface that was true, I guess, but behind the scenes when all tired and wary parents are home snuggled in their beds fast asleep, these pillars of the community are out pillaging the "Hill" community. And the pièce de résistance, the site A Capehart community usually supplied most of the party drinks by way unbeknownst to them, at least until morning when they found their beer missing from the garage refrigerator. Yep! You got it, although, this was just mainly during our junior and senior years of 1965 and 1966, as if that means anything, mostly during the late summer nights that most of this partying occurred.

Mr. Perfect everything, Steve Metcalf wasn't nicknamed "Dog-Man" because he liked puppies. Mike "Kinna" Kinne wasn't really going to take after his Dads legal officer position, and Gary Whitnack wasn't the Little Teddy Bear he was made out to be. James "Pokey" Bowman, oh my god! He was ready for anything in the pillaging category, along with the Martin boys, mainly Roger and me and on occasion Duke and the Sorge brothers, Bobby and Dikes. All who, at this special time, lived in the Capehart A territory. This didn't exclude other friends from other areas of the valley who would also enjoy these summer night excursions, including many of the local area girl friends who enjoyed a good summer night party. You notice I rarely mention them by name? Hmm, I guess I've just always been kind to the ladies!! Ha-ha

To get out late at night, say after midnight Roger and I had it down pretty well. Still in bunk beds we would make up dummies with pillows and blankets to make our, what we called "ME'S". "Roger, check my ME and I'll check yours" was usually the last words before we slipped out the unscreened window of our bedroom to head out to meet up with others for that nights adventure and for the refreshments, which had already been pinpointed (ID'ED) earlier that day as we looked for opened garages that had refrigerators for us to tip toe in and retrieve the nights party drinking cocktails. We called this pre-partying venture "tipping." Who ever got the goods would bring them to the designated place. I remember one night, Bowman's parents were out of town for the week, so we were partying at Bowman's house up on Blueridge and Pokey was out "Tipping" with, I think Whitnack, and the next thing we know here they come up Kearsarge rolling a fifteen gallon keg of beer toward Pokey's house. I believe that keg took care of several parties that weekend for so many partyers and still had left overs come Monday!

Kinna (Mike Kinne) told a funny story of one time when the party was at Metcalf's house back over on Wasp Road, and Kinna had been tipping and found a good refer where he retrieved a case of beer over on Kearsarge and was running back through the Richmond School playground late on a dark night, thinking the six-foot-high chain link fence was just on the other side of the tree ditch row, closer to Wasp road. Well, it was on his side of the tree ditch, and he ran smack dab into it going full speed while holding a case of beer over his head. It didn't knock him out and he was able to retrieve all the cans of beer spread out all over the tree ditch, but at the party, he had red chain link fence squares all over his face and arms which later turned black and blue for several days! Yep, crazy summer days.

I'll never forget one very early summer morning Roger and I had just come back through the window and taking down our "ME'S" to get in bed, when my mom came in to wake up Roger, forgetting it was his turn that week to serve 6 A.M. mass at church. Now, this might help make more since as I continue referring to "Mom's Little Angels," referring to us Martin boys, mainly Roger and me. As I have talked about before, my Mom is a very devout Catholic and her family, with the lord's help, was going to grow up the same. This did include each of her seven little angels, at the age of eight becoming Alter Boys. Yep, and to make it even tougher back at that time, mass was in Latin. Every one of us were Alter boys for at least five or six years.

Anyways, Roger says, "Mom, I'm not feeling well," so she feels his head and said "Yeah, you are warm and a bit sweaty." "Richard," meaning Duke. "Wake up, Roger's not feeling well and you need to serve mass for him this morning" as she walked out of the room. Duke jumps out of his bunk, loudly complaining that "No shit he's warm, he just got done running home from out all night," and Roger jumps out of bed and popped Duke in the nose and told him to shut the fuck up and help him out. Yep, and after Duke cleaned the blood from his nose went off with Mom to serve mass for Roger! Oh, what brothers won't do for each other!

Serious accidents were a rarity in those days on Base to the Martin family. It can't get any worse than losing a child or family member as we did in 1958, living on Rowe street. The family did experience another serious one several years later when we lived up on the Hill at 214 Shangri-La Circle, although not as devastating but very serious.

Let me set the stage; my mom is certainly old school from the mountains of West Virginia when it comes to cooking and baking. I mean she made so many things from scratch, especially around the holidays as when this accident happened. This time Mom was making homemade noodle soup in the kitchen. I happened to have been in the kitchen with her, along with my brother Duke as we were rolling out dough, thinning it into sheets to cut up into thin noodle strips, maybe ten inches long for the soup broth that Mom has boiling in her large pressure cooker on the stove. Well, apparently Mom didn't realize she hadn't tightened or latch down the clamp on one side of the pressure cooker that kept the lid firmly and safely tight as the soup broth boiled inside. She was no more than a few feet, with her back turned from the cooker, and I was maybe a few feet further, on the other side of her, when the pressure got so high it finally blew the lid right off the unsecured cooker, shooting scolding hot soup all over the kitchen and the back of my Mom, from the shoulders down her butt and legs! I think Duke was out of the kitchen at that exact time, but I also got splashed on the right foot and leg. We really at the time didn't realize the seriousness of the burns Mom received, as it wasn't something you could see at first, just redness, but we got her out the back door and into the snow that was fortunately on the ground from a recent snow storm, as we packed her back up and down with snow. Still not realizing the severity of this type of burns, we immediately got her to Drummond Medical while all the time keeping snow on the burns. Thankfully we kept the cold snow on the burns and as quick as we did as the doctor said that certainly helped her from going into shock! Trust me, gods hand came into play providing the unusual snow storm!

Very naïve still of the situation and thinking she'll be coming home with us that night. The doctor finally explained the severity of her burns. My mom had been placed in the Intensive Care Unit (ICU) on her face under 24/7 watch. She had third degree burns on approximately 30 percent of her body, mainly her back side! Just the sting and pain from the blisters I had received on my foot, I can't even imagine what kind of pain she was experiencing! I mean, they wouldn't let anyone, not even family, see or visit her for the first five days of isolation. Finally, family were permitted to visit, only if dressed in the protective garb from head to toe protecting her from infection. Hell, that's all we were able to do is see her, as they had her knocked out with morphine, saving her from the intense pain from the burns. We finally got her home some three weeks after she entered the hospital. She had some pretty damaging tissue damage and scaring down her back from this terrible accident. Thank god for the snow that hit the base that week. Lessons learned!

On a more positive note, while I'm talking about Moms family recipes from West Virginia, besides the wonderful homemade noddle soup, was another very special holiday, made from scratch recipe that my whole family and most of our friends looked forward to every November. A delicacy that still today is a family favorite, a delight enjoyed over the past sixty plus years. We called my Moms West Virginia family recipe "Grits." NO, nothing like the oatmeal type grits you find in the deep southern states of our country, not even close! Our family Grits, made in a very large pot or as we called it "A Batch," and included the main ingredients of pork, beef, onions and plenty of oats and spices, made into solid lofts (ten to twelve large lofts per batch) and frozen until ready to eat. Once defrosted, a loft is sliced up into thin 4-inch slices and fried until crispy brown and enjoyed with catchup, mainly for breakfast. A large loft would feed breakfast for seven big eaters like we had in our family, a batch would always get us through the Christmas holidays. Very healthy for a large growing Martin family on Base in the fifties and sixties. Today, my kids, grandkids and many friends refer to them as "Grand Mary's Grits" and look forward several times a year for my new batch...

Anyway, getting back to base housing, the last of the territory's on base of course the "Hill" community, even though the Capehart A was considered on "The Hill." I'm talking about those first on Base Senior Officer Quarters (SOQ) pink brick housing where a lot of military families lived, but also, a lot of high GS rated civilian families of which most had been permanent residents for many years, much different from their military counterparts who usually were on Base for a three-to-four-year tour of duty. I knew some of these long time Base civilian's living on the Hill such as Dr. Calloday, one of the base scientists and such a great guy to all kids on Base. I believe Doc also became the technical director at some point and lived in the first house next to the Officers Club with his family including son Johnny, brother Dukes age, and Johnny's tenacious older sister Carolyn, who was a year older than Roger.

Also, just a house or two down from the Calloday's lived a civilian legal officer, Hal Byrd, and his somewhat large family who I happened to have gotten to know very well. Especially during the summer of 65' as I dated the oldest of the Byrd's family, Kathy, who was a year older than me! There was also oldest son Billy and Jimmy, both close to my age, very good friends of mine. As with Kathy, they were at many of the summer parties. And youngest brother Bobby, plus one or two other sisters. I must say that was a very interesting family!

In the middle of the SOQ housing was what we called The Captain's Field, a large grassy area the size of a football field surrounded by large shade trees. Over many years it was known that there was a lot of, let's just say, "Making out" up there on that ole Captain's field. In another SOQ just on the northeast side of the Captains field lived the pretty Susan Swanson and two other sisters, the daughters of a Navy pilot. Susan, a friend our age (and still a friend today) and another Ms. Little League that will be mentioned later.

I really didn't know back in those days the Wherry Housing territory and the two hundred or so duplex housing nor the streets very well. Located out the back gate in its own little community. I did get to know many of the kids that lived there as they were a part of the Base and went to the on Base schools and activities like we all did. From my class friends like Donna Martin, not related but to this day we still call each other, "Cuz." Also, Tom "Big T" Mather, who I had become very close with since high school, his brothers, Jerry and Randy, and sister Sandy, who I became good friends with in high school. I also remember their dad Bob, who also, besides working on the Base, owned and drove an ice cream truck, mainly during summer days up and down the streets of the Base, many times with Tommy riding along helping serve ice cream bars! There was also Jeff and sister Kay Walker, both the same age as me, and if twins, well, let's just say they didn't look like each other! We all three went to many elementary schools and high school together! These are just a few names off the top of my head I remember, but I know there were so many more that I went through many different schools or sports together but just that I didn't realize they lived in Off-Base Wherry housing.

In my attempt to describe each housing territory and mentioning **just a few** of my good friends and other kids I knew and grew up with from each of their territories, in school, or elsewhere on Base. I hoped to have emphasized the closeness of the thousands of youths that were living in this small housing community on board this huge military base and how easy it was for all these thousands of kids to get to know each other. The friends I mention and talk about, I have been friends with since the early days at China Lake and as I am still today. There were thousands more kids I knew fairly well or knew who they were but just didn't add or from my lack of memory to remember! Still today I run into many that I haven't mentioned here, and we'd always stop to visit and no doubt talk about something fun from our past at China Lake.

Outside of the Base, throughout the country, could any other kids that grew up in the late fifties and early sixties in their own little town or city have the ability to say they still communicate, have knowledge or good friends with hundreds of the kids they grew up with. I doubt they even knew that many kids, or more so, communicate with, some 70 years later!

Wouldn't it be an interesting read if every kid growing up on Base during this same time frame, the late fifties and early sixties, would write their personal experiences about their neighborhood territory and the friends they grew up with and ventures they experienced along the way. Now, again, remember I'm talking about thousands of kids. I would bet most of their stories would all be of the same "common" topics, only in their own story or version of each experience.

I'll give you an example. Let's use a "Place" say, "Base Theater." All these thousands of kids that grew up on base, every last one of them, some much more than others, went to the "Base Theater," typically referred to as "The Show" or "The Movies" and usually together with family and/or friends, each would have stories of their own about the Base Theater and their personal version of those experiences. I know just for our gang of guys from our territory, we had hundreds of experiences through the years going to, coming from, and even during a Movie!

CHAPTER 5
The School District

Every September brought the beginning of the new school year on Base. It seemed as if there was a school for every neighborhood territory in the community. As I rekindle thoughts of all the different schools I attended, going through the school years while growing up on Base during the fifties and sixties, I think it would be of interest to illustrate the school system and how it worked for all the kids, as compared to other towns or cities, including Ridgecrest, where typically every kid would go to the same school with the same kids and same friends all their school life, K-12 or K-8 and then four years in high school. China Lake schools, where all these thousands of kids growing up on Base from different neighborhood territories, demonstrated how easy it was starting up new friendships, whatever the age, at each different school. If not actually friends, at least you knew each other by name. Knowing so many kids for so long, mainly from attending so many different schools, with so many different kids throughout their school life, certainly increased our friendship list.

So as an example, let's just take my school life as I grew up through school to illustrate where and how I was able to get to know so many of the Base kids along the way. Also, just as a note, many of the times but not always, my two brothers, Roger and Duke, as the three of us were close in age would usually attend the same school.

As I mentioned, come September was the beginning of the school year; I must also mention come early June was the last day of school and the beginning of summer. The last day of school also brings back memories of what was kind of a fad, at least for the Rowe Street Gang and a lot of the kids of other neighborhood territories. As the students leaving their current grade school for the last time on that last day of school with the anticipation of going into the next grade level come September, we wanted to help this anticipation, both boys and girls, with a reminder by writing a large number representing the next grade level on their forehead with dark red lipstick. Just another mischievous little thing we had to do! I have no idea, or at least remember exactly why we did this helpful deed or even when it started, like a carry down from the older kids, but as I recall, we did it for many years! There weren't very many kids that didn't get this forehead reminder!

Basically, starting my school life at 58-A Rowe and in the Rowe Street neighborhood territory, there were several schools. The first was Vewieg Elementary School at the far west end of Rowe street and where I went to 2nd & 4th grades. I can't remember anything about 2nd grade. On the other hand, I remember quite a bit of the 3rd grade. In 3rd grade I went to another Rowe Street elementary school named Rowe St. School, located back down Rowe and just across the street from Bobby and Dikes (Sorge's) house. As I recall, Rowe St School was 1st through 6th grade and where I became much closer friends with many of my age kids from the Langley, Independence, and Hornet street housing territories.

Rowe street assembly

As I mentioned before, Karen Marker was kind of my girlfriend in 3rd grade as we went through the school year together, along with many of her gang of girls and the guys that lived around her on Independence St. I'll never forget our 3rd grade teacher, Miss Fincher. She couldn't have been older than early 20's, and besides being a really nice teacher, she was absolutely beautiful, at least to me. My Mom would joke for years later that I had her buy me a ring to give to Miss Fincher. No shit, I mean I used to pull weeds in her yard and little helpful shit like that! Had to have been my first little boy crush!

Another event, I guess you could call it, that still sticks in my memories from in 3rd grade was the Monday I brought a Chuckawalla to school that I had caught the past weekend up on B Mountain. I had it in a box and showing it off on the playground at lunch time when the little bitch grabbed hold of my middle finger, and that was it. I mean if you ever been bitten by a Chuck, then you know they don't let go! We started heading up to the nurse's office for help as this big sucker, maybe 20 inches long, hung from my finger. Trust me, they ain't a pretty lizard! Just about at the office, we looked back, and I swear every frick-in kid at school was behind us as we made it into the nurse's office. Holy shit, I thought the nurse was going to faint when I lifted my hand for help with this big ugly lizard hanging from my finger, as she supplied us a pair of pliers to pry its mouth open to release me. Funny as shit... as I said, I remember 3rd and 4th grades pretty darn well.

Remember the fire drills?

It was around my fourth-grade time period that I really got into playing marbles. That's right, marbles! As I think back, marbles was more of a boy's game, although I'm sure a few of the girls played. I just can't recall playing marbles with the girls! In 4th grade, maybe, what eight, nine years old, the girls were still playing with dolls and just trying to annoy boys! I know all the Rowe street guys collected and played marbles as well as so many other guys for a few years around the Base. As I remember, there was really only two games of marbles we played.

One easy game I believed we called Chase-em, I could be wrong about that, but it doesn't matter. Two guys would each take turns chasing one another's marble, shooting his marble at the others guys, back and forth until one hit's the other guy's marble. So, he wins that match and gets to keep the guy's marble. This is why it is important to collect marbles, you can lose them faster than you collect them. The other marble game I remember was the Circle game. You would draw in the dirt, or chalk on the asphalt or concrete, a large circle. The size depended how many guys are playing. Let's just say four guys playing would call for a circle maybe four or five feet in diameter. All the players would put in the middle of the circle or pot, say ten marbles each, then the four guys would flip to brake or go first. Without coming inside the circle just on the brake, each guy would shoot with their personal "shooter" and keep all marbles he knocks out of the circle. If he doesn't knock a marble out of the circle, then it's the next guys turn. The winner would be the guy who got the most marbles!

There was a lot more to playing marbles than what I've described, I mean that's just the games. The marbles themselves and how to shoot them was a huge part of the game. I mean there were guys who were experts in the fucking game. Had all the great shooters like Aggies, Purees, and even Bulls Eye Agates, the primo of all marbles! Some of the best shooters were guys that just couldn't miss, had great shooting ability, and won and collected thousands of these little fricking marbles! Hey, you guys ever remember playing marbles?

4th Grade Square Dancing

One other event, as I think back to 4th grade at Vieweg School, was the district started having boys and girls doing things together, like as partners. Here in 4th grade, we were introduced to square dancing. Goofy at first, for sure, but for me, I actually liked it and participated quit often in many square dance events. We always had a new cowboy shirt and jeans, and the girls would have their new western looking, wide dresses.

The Rowe Street Gang hung around Vieweg School a lot since it was close by our homes, but more importantly, it had nice wide concrete walkways with some downhill runs in and out through the school buildings, perfect for roller-skating. Now back in the fifties and early sixties, roller skates were made with steel wheels, I mean, hit a pebble and your gone head first! We all got damn good on skates as we played roller derby on the walks in and out around the school buildings, trying to maintain as we whipped around corners racing each other, knowing to crash would result in some definite bleeding. As we got older and more daring, like nine or ten years old, we took the steel wheels off both sides of the skate and attached them to a two-by-four maybe sixteen inches long and taught ourselves how to skate on top of the two-by-four wood skate. I mean, we could just haul ass on this piece of wood, just gliding like a boat on water, but again with the steel wheels, when you hit just a little pebble, your shit's gone! I mean like going down a steep hill at what felt like 20 miles an hour and BAM, hit a pebble, and you're flying but without the skateboard...we did get pretty damn good on those wood skateboards. I mean I could even do a handstand and stay up for some 100 feet or so. The Rowe Street Gang could do it all.

In 5th grade, as we grew older, we became more interested in, let's just say, "The opposite sex." I spent the school year at Groves School, located between Hornet and Groves streets, just across the street from Al Hyles house on Groves. Fifth grade at Groves brought many more kids my age together, including some I knew and was friends with from Little League. Kids like Albert, Steve Troy, and Charlie Walker, who were two new guys, I started running with during this time period! Also, others from the "Tomac Housing Territory" such as Gordy Irvin, Herbie Pinto, Eddie Lusher, and Al Senn. Plus, a new kid on the Rowe Street block, Tommy Beede, who lived two doors down on the west side from me and became one of my best friends for several years, before his family moved to San Diego.

Life at this age and beyond, with all these bandits, had begun to get hilariously interesting to say the least! Anyway, the best memory at 5th grade Groves

School was one that we all, mainly guys, still talk and joke about today. Now keep in mind the girls at this age are starting to show signs of female development, but there was one girl through our 5th grade class who was fully developed, I mean, as much as a grown woman in her twenty's. I won't get into a lot of detail of the things she'd let us do, with consent of course. I mean us stupid guys, the truth be, we hadn't a clue at this age how to really do anything sexual. I mean, none of us young green horns knew shit, but she'd let us play around with anything and anywhere we wanted, as she just giggled. It's kind of weird, as she was a nice girl and personable throughout the school year, just for some reason she had these permissive ways! Strange for sure.

Well, unfortunately, it got around all over school and finally to the principal. I have to admit the school handled this sensitive issue fairly well and just really educated us through the reproduction system and the difference and right and wrong of sex. Of course, us big shots just laughed it off and pranced around like we "know how to do it." Yeah, right! The worst part, before it all came tumbling down, was that over at the high school, word got out and some of the high school pricks tried to get some of the action, and of course they weren't just playing around like us young dumb fucks. These guys, from what I understood at the time, had a little line outside her house, which was only a few blocks from the school. I must admit, I didn't understand this mentality and actually kind of felt a little sad for her, most likely more than she did for herself, as she just seemed to enjoy all the excitement! Geez! One for the memory files for sure!

As I continued on to the next level into 6th grade, the first half of my 6th grade was back at Rowe Street School, and again, with some of the old same age friends and some new ones, until just after Christmas, then the school district moved all 6th graders from all the schools throughout the Base into some new Quonset Huts turned into classrooms at Murray School, just the other side of the school where all the 7th and 8th graders attended jr. high school. A move that was kind of scary being around the bigger kids for many, but for me and a few other guys, well, we knew and ran with a lot of the older guys over the years, like my brother Roger, so no big deal. Murray school was the first school that every kid on Base at the school level of 7th & 8th grade would attend and for us guys was really the first introduction of little girls transforming into young women, unless you came from 5th grade Groves school.

I remember in 7th grade at Murray one cold early winter morning just as I arrived at the basketball courts Gordy, Herbie, Albert, and a few other guys were hanging around a frozen puddle of water on the asphalt court and taking turns running and sliding, trying to stay standing-up on the ice. I jumped in and said, "Let me show you how it's done." Yep, that was the last thing I remember until I woke up some hour or so later looking up at Nurse McLean looking at me with a terrifying look on her face and my dad and his friend Chuck Mangle standing next to her. Nurse "La V" McLean, of course, was the wife of the technical director of the base and the inventor and main scientist/physicist in the development of the notorious Sidewinder missile, Dr. Bill McLean. Well, that little mishap cost me a week at home under watchful eyes of my mom and daily calls from Nurse McLean.

Jr. high school really brought us guys even closer together as we were introduced to team competition in basketball and flag football at two different levels in both 7th and 8th grade, lightweight and heavyweight. Our PE teachers were always the coaches. Mr. McGinnis, or as we all called him "Mugsy," was the 8th grade coach, and, at least during my two years, Mr. Rocky Gardner was the 7th grade coach, and both were no-nonsense coaches and the PE teachers. Oh shit! those two guys loved to give ass whooping if you fucked-up around school. Well, it certainly was a deterrent those two coaches with their long, wooden paddles they kept in their desk. I know it just took once for me as that ass whooping paddle hurt like shit, I mean like "crying hurt," as I tried holding my breath while bent over, hugging the desk! Didn't need to tell me twice.

Mrs. McLean, besides being the school nurse, was also the girls PE teacher and a good friend (respectfully) with the girls, although us guys thought she was cool too. Every day at lunch she'd open up the girls PE hut for all the kids to come in to visit and dance while the loud music played and heard across campus. The girls nick-named this noon event "The Campus Corner." Of course, 99 percent of the dancing was the girls dancing with each other, at least until the guys started having girlfriends, then you had to dance! Yep, where it all started! I'll tell ya', these young sweeties had us guys by our peach-fuzz balls.

My 8th grade came and went as fast as my 7th grade year. The guys started growing and developing physically in coordination, in weight and height, and all over our private parts, sort of to speak! Playing sports, girls, and going to school was the only thing it seemed there was on earth as this testosterone level thing ravished our little boy bodily system like "stink on shit." In my 8th grade homeroom, Mr. Willie's class, there was, once again, a bunch of us screw-up's, guys that I have become close friends with along the way through school and sports.

I remember one day in homeroom I had a broken big toe from some sporting activity and couldn't put my shoe or sock on. I mean it was all swollen and black & blue and hurt like shit. Mr. Willie let me stay in the class room during lunch to keep my foot up while he went to lunch. No fucking sooner than he left, here comes Gordy, Albert, and Raymond Hayton into the room and over to where I'm sitting. Albert grabs my arms behind me and Gordy and Hayton start putting super glue all over my throbbing toe and then dumping sawdust all over the glue. Real nice, I mean how am I going to get that shit off my toe. Fucking Gordy and Albert always pulling something! To make it even worse, Mr. Willie just laughed about it when he got back. Some crazy days back in 8th grade. Knucklehead stuff, ya' know!

There was one other episode in Mr. Willie's class in 8th grade that has always been a topic of conversation among the participants of this venture. In these classrooms at Murray school there were large metal air vent boxes for the heating and A/C systems for each classroom. When looking down through the vents of these units it was dark with no end, like just drops off into darkness, very suspicious to us wondering pirates. So Gordy, me, and Albert, I believe, decided to investigate further. So the day we went in, we brought a flashlight with us. We waited until Mr. Willie went to lunch and we unscrewed the vent. We went feet first into the air vent duct, which wasn't even a duct but just dropped off into black space.

Actually, this really took balls, I mean not knowing where in this dark space we were dropping into. It turned out to be about 10-foot-deep drop, landing on a concrete floor, actually, pretty scary not knowing where the hell we were! With the flashlight we could see we were in a huge tunnel with concrete floors and walls that went several different ways, so with no way getting back up the A/C vent, we started walking around and finally found some double doors, which of course were locked. We pounded on the doors and finally a janitor heard us and opened the doors. Yep, straight to the principal's office!

Well, what we thought was going to be our parents called and a defiant suspension, turned out to be very educational. What we found was a very large and long set of tunnels that the district would use as a bomb shelter if ever needed below the school. The school district decided, actually a good idea, thinking it was important enough for all the rest of the kids in school, to have an assembly for the whole school, both seventh and eighth graders, about the bomb shelter beneath the school, what it was for, and then gave all the kids a tour of the actual tunnels. The easy way rather than how we had found it just a week before! Pretty interesting shit, I must say. Yep, eighth grade at Murray Jr. High, China Lake, California! Defiantly a fun year!

The last four years of my Base school life would be in high school and actually wasn't even on Base but in Ridgecrest. At the beginning of the Base, as I mentioned, the first Burroughs High School was what is now 7th and 8th grade Murray Jr. High school, up until around 1959 or so, when the School district built the new Burroughs High School on property that bordered the southern end of the base, approximately a half mile south through the desert from my house on Rowe street, just between Rowe and the base Wherry Housing community. It was built on Ridgecrest land and only about a five-minute walk from my home at 58-A Rowe street on Base.

Of course, along with the new high school, the Base built a guard shack, just like the Main front gate and the Richmond Road back gate, and yes, you needed your Base pass to get through, even just to go to school! It was part of life for all of us and was just no big deal, typical stuff living on Base. I believe my brother Dave was in the first graduating class from the new Burroughs of Ridgecrest. I have to say I don't have very many memories of the Burroughs (Burros) playing football at the old BHS complex, now Murray school's Kelly Field, not like I have at the current school location in Ridgecrest. I do recall much more watching the Burros basketball and Dave play at their old home facility, the Base gym, a block north from the then Burroughs High School.

Oh lord! I remember playing as kids on the Kelly Field. Hell, who doesn't remember Kelly Field! Centrally located right there at Murray School, it was such a great place to play around as kids growing up on our Base. Its large concrete monument with a large missile like bullet on top in memory of the athlete, John Kelly. Many times a bunch of us guys would get together for our own little pick-up football games mainly in the winter months during football season, and of course, imitate our local heroes, those older high school varsity players during our pickup games.

I just loved Kelly Field, named after John Kelly, who from everything I heard was a varsity MVP type football player his senior year at Old Burros (Murray), who lost his life in a car accident on a trip to Kernville during his senior year.

The Kelly award continues to this day over at the Burroughs of Ridgecrest campus. I didn't know or remember watching John Kelly play, as it was before I could remember, but I certainly knew the Kelly Field that was named in his honor.

All the thousands of kids growing up at China Lake back in those early years remembered playing and enjoying the well maintained, green grass of Kelly Field. Memories of looking east over the Dry Lake and seeing the B Mountain, with its huge "B" at its base, through the desert, representing the beloved high school, especially during winter nights, as the Base annually would power up generators to light up our very large, well-lit Christmas star over the big "B" in honor of the Christmas holiday season for all to see across the valley. I can remember so many times playing tackle or touch pickup football games on weekends or holidays with many friends or with the Murray Jr. High School flag football team, where we played all our home games through two years of junior high school.

How about just walking with thousands of other adults and kids over to Kelly Field's green grass after Little Leagues all afternoon and early evening special 4th of July baseball activities at Shuffle field and all the little league fields? Everyone settling on the grassy field, laying out blanket, sitting with family, buddies or your girlfriend to watch and enjoy the China Lake fire department 4th of July Fire Works display on the dry Mirror Lake to end the day. What a great time in China Lake sports, at least for us very young kids around my age with all our memories of our heroes, these older high school guys, who, in my opinion, were great local athletes, including my brother Dave, John McLaughlin, Ronnie Marker, Ron Melia, Gary Maxwell, John Penny, Jimmy Breaw, Clyde Griffin, Glen Crowson, Mike Baker, Gary and Bobby Kohler, Mike Mamula, John Dunaway, and Tommy Tally. Also, the great Short Brothers, Bob and Roger, just loved those guys and so many other older guys at Burros sports that so inspired us local kids growing up on Base.

When I say older, I'm talking like maybe six to ten years older when we were around 5th, 6th, and 7th graders. Back in those days the only other sports heroes we had were the professionals and some highly publicly totted college players. Heroes like Mickey Mantle, Sandy Kofax, and many of the likes. Back then us little guys, us gamers only had our local high school varsity standouts, from football on Kelly Field to basketball at the Base gym and then later on over to the new Burroughs gym and football field on the Burroughs in Ridgecrest campus, where it is today.

Well, now, here I am talking so much about our local sports hero's as kids growing up watching at high school games, I'm feeling a little guilty not mentioning the pretty cheerleaders and song-leaders of Burros during those same games, as we little girl watchers gawked at them the same, if not more than our heroes playing the game on the field! Oh yeah, that testosterone was kicking in even back then! I still remember a few around my brother Dave's age that come, very easily to mind. Okay, for us young and horny little desert rats, the few that stood out from those days, beauties I remember such as Jinx Grell, Stephanie Van Hagan, Rita Allen, Margrett Appleton, Sharon Mamula, and my all-time favorite Deloris Burke.

1959 "Homecoming Queen" Deloris Burke

Jinx, Rita, and Stephanie (Middle three)

After completion of my exciting two years of jr. high school at on base Murray, the school districts, as they have done since the new Burroughs was built in Ridgecrest, combined all the 8th graders in the Indians Wells Valley (IWV), including Murray and the two junior highs located in Ridgecrest, Monroe Jr. High, and the few 8th graders from the small Saint Ann's Catholic school. Introducing each year's new group of eighth graders from throughout the valley as the new freshman class at Burroughs High School. The lowest class on the totem pole and, oh boy, did the upper classes let us know and took advantage of it. The move from Murray Junior High to high school was the biggest move of my school life, as I'm sure it was for all the new freshman coming to high school.

Oh my gosh, I've never seen so many pretty grown girls in my life in the same school. As I mentioned, the upper classman took advantage of the incoming freshmen, but I was lucky, I mean really lucky! A senior girl, cheerleader and, I believe, homecoming queen, the pretty Margret Appleton, who I got to know very well, and I became good friends as she was the girlfriend of my old little league pitching coach, very well-known Burros alumni, Gary Maxwell, who I had the utmost respect for as we became very close, good friends since Little league as we are still today.

Anyway, it was during what they called Hell Week or Slave Week, something like that, where the freshman would have to do chores and other little duties during the first week of school, should an upper classman request you as their slave. Well, precious Margret (I'm sure encouraged by Gary) chose me to be her slave for the week, had me the whole week meet her after each of her classes and carry her books with her to her next class. If that wasn't enough, it was mandatory that I kissed her on the cheek before she'd go into each class. Damn! I had it rough through hell week, I mean pure hell!

My freshmen class became the class of 66' for the next four years. Yeah, a tough-ass class, no bias, huh? Except for sports and academic competition between the two junior high schools back in 7th and 8th, we personally really didn't know much about these freshman kids from Monroe. They all lived in Ridgecrest and us Murray kids on Base, and remember, nobody could get on base unless you had a Base pass as proof you lived on base or have a visitor's pass called in for you. Really our first introduction was being here in high school, not to say over the years we didn't know of each other or heard about one another and actually did get along, mainly for us guys through sports, which also included eyeballing the Monroe cheerleaders of course, as the Monroe guys did our cheerleaders. However, until high school, we really didn't see the Ridgecrest kids. Oh, but it didn't take long before everybody was a BHS student and the Class of 66' became very close and good friends, not only with each other but with all the other students from all the other classes at Burroughs as we became just another part of the group or family of the many teenagers in the Indian Wells Valley going to the same school. Making so many more longtime friends forever!

My class of 66 Cheerleaders

My class of 66 Songleaders

Actually, the Base kids and Ridgecrest kids really did become close, as I'm sure it was in any high school that the incoming freshmen became just a part of the four year high school process. I really think more so in our case, maybe because of the same desert environment that all the kids grew up in, and after the freshman year, it really didn't matter from where anybody came. I remember so well what was in my mind my first few days at high school. I mean, there was so many beautiful, so well-defined young ladies going to Burroughs High, not just from the different junior high schools but from all over the valley, including Red Mountain, Inyokern, and other desert communities.

As my high school years came to an end as part of the class of 1966, I have to add one last story that occurred the last week of high school, similar to the first week in my freshmen year during Hell Week four years prior, it involves pretty ladies. This story I will never forget nor does one of my best friends, who experienced the adventure with me. Let me set the stage by backing up a little and explain the players involved. Of course, yours truly and one of my best friends, still today some 55+ years later, Tom Kleine, Aka; Da-Tooms. Now Tom and I went through little league together, high school basketball and were both members of the Catholic Youth Organization (CYO) and its very good basketball team we had during our time. Tom's parents, John and Anita were also devout Catholic's and close friends with my parents. All the

Kleine' kids (6) went to St Ann's catholic school in Ridgecrest until high school. After Tom's eighth grade year at St Ann's Tom along with another friend, John Weber decided to go to the Catholic Seminary in Fresno to begin the process of becoming priest. Three years later Tom was back at Burroughs his junior year with no further interest in the priesthood, never losing his intense, interest in sports but he also gained a whole new perspective in the opposite sex. I'm sure making up for lost time from three years in the Seminary!! Ha-ha...

Fast forward back to last week of our senior year and Tom and I decide not to go with the Senior class to Disneyland, as every senior class in Southern California did every year. No, we decided to head out on our own to Newport Beach, a place over the last several years that was a very popular destination for a lot of Southern California kids, including many of us from China Lake/Ridgecrest, especially during Easter vacation. No doubt instigated by the Beach Boys madness that hit the country in the early sixties. I'm sure I could write several chapters just on those adventures traveling to Newport beach as teenagers with guys like; Kinna (Mike Kinne) Whitnack, Metcalf, of course Roger, Gordy, Albert and Herbie, and so many other groups from our area. A beach party time for sure!!

Anyway; Tom and I arrived down in Newport beach in mid-morning and checked into a "drive up in front of your room type motel" and as we're un-packing our car, a very nice convertible pulled in right next to our car space with two, very attractive older women. As they un-packed their car we exchanged pleasantries and they seemed really very personable as we visited out-front of the two rooms, we both were thinking, "my god what beautiful older women" I mean they had to be mid to late twenties. I know I was thinking, "I'd give my left arm for a taste of these ripe tomato's". Yeah right, dream on dude!! After a few minutes of a very nice chat with the older ladies from next door we headed to the beach for some great body surfing and fun & sun on the beach. I bet during that afternoon Tom and I handed out two dozen papers with our motel address and announcing party tonight starting at 7pm. I also will bet not one paper invitation was given to a guy, nope, all girls. Ha-ha ha...Yep, should be a fun time tonight!! After a great afternoon playing on the beach, we decided we'd better get going so we could prepare for our little shindig tonight. We stopped off at a grocery store we passed on the way and bought some bags of chips and dip, a few bags of ice and a case of beer. So, at checkout the beer didn't go over to well as the guy asked for ID and neither of us could show proof. After a little leisure and admonishment from the grocer we left with just the Ice, chips, and shit. We have tons of girls coming to our party and we don't have any fucking booze!! "Now what" as we set debating, with our door opened in our motel room, hotter than crap from the shitty air-conditioner as the afternoon continued getting later. Just around four o'clock our friendly women friends pulled up to their room from their day at the beach. Hmm, I said to Tooms, this may be our last chance to resolve this dilemma, we went next door and knocked on our women neighbor's door! We explained that we were hosting a party tonight and have a bunch of kids coming over and we weren't able to buy the beer. "you guys want us to buy you your beer for your party tonight" said the much shorter black hair lady as she looked over at her taller blonde hair partner, they both started laughing. I said "Yes ma'am" and the shorter black hair lady said "How cute is that. Yeah sure, we'll buy your beer for you guys" as they both continued laughing, they really seemed to get a kick being these boys' buyer!! So, we gave them $20.00 dollars for a case of beer and off they went. Within fifteen minutes they were back with our beer. We told them thanks, that you've saved our party and told them they were welcome to come over, even though it will just be a bunch of kids. The tall blonde lady said "oh how sweet is that, we have plans ourselves but you just never know we may just drop by." As they both laughed to each other again.

By seven o'clock Tom and I were ready to get the show on the road as we pulled our first pull-top off our Budweiser's. The front door opened so no one can miss the party in side! Eight-thirty, two buds later and still, no chicks! Damn, what the hell. Tom suggested going down to the beach walk and see what was going on before we drink too much and shouldn't be driving. I agreed, and so we drove down to 54th street pier area where there was a lot of music and crowds of kids dancing and partying. We stayed down there a few hours parting and telling kids about the party at our motel but just couldn't get any takers to break away from their fun and come up to a dungy old motel. Actually, I couldn't blame them. So, after a few hours of some fun partying at the beach, it was maybe ten-thirty or so we decided to head on back to the room, in hopes of some of the many girls we told about the party would actually show up. Feeling NO pain as we both sat in the room chatting like a couple girls at slumber party, determined not to let all this beer go to waste, with still the slightest hope for some late party goers showing up. Around eleven o'clock we heard a car pull up out front and people closing their car doors as we bubbled with excitement hoping for some partyers and then we heard the door open next door and realized it was the old ladies coming back from their night out. Oh well, just a quick high to a low again!! Until; knock, knock, knock at our door! "Hmm, what do we have here?" I said with excitement as I opened the door. To are amazement it was our women friends from next door, somewhat giggly but wobblier with a bottle of wine in each of their hands. " How'd your party turn out tonight fellas, from the looks of it, it just got here!" The tall blonde said with a very sexy, fun laugh as they both made their way into our room!!

Now, that's all I have to say about how special the rest of our evening went. these two special ladies were the nicest and most fun ladies that Tom and I had ever experienced. I honestly don't even remember their names; I mean we're talking 55 years ago. Just for fun, I have named them after two cheer/song leaders from the class of 65. Julie, the shorter, black hair beauty, maybe 5'4" dark tan and a very firm body, I mean tight. The taller blonde, I've named Janet, maybe just under six foot tall, also very tan and very well defined and also very firm. They both were from San Diego and worked together for Sea World as mermaids in the Parks large aquarium pools and had just started a weeks' vacation from their work. Very pretty ladies!!

I so remember driving back home to China Lake the following day in Toms dads old ford sedan, Tom had picked up a couple of large cigars while gassing up in Newport and here we were on Hwy. 14 heading through the Newhall mountain area just above the Antelope Valley, just cruising along with me at the wheel and Tooms lighting up the two Gar's and hands me one. With tiny red panties on my head, a souvenir Julie gave me to remember her buy and the both of us toking on the large cigars just cruising down the highway reminiscing about our high school life and what a "fantasy come true" last day of school to remember our wonderful high school years at Burroughs!! Tooms looks over at me, his bare feet on the dash board, blows a poof of smoke out from his Gar and with a silly grin says; "JJ (his nick name for me) if life gets better than this, we're in for a hell of a future." I said, "Beyond the High Sierra's" my Tooms..

JJ & Da Tooms

CHAPTER 6
Baseball, America's Game

As we dive into baseball and the wonderful memories of Little League at China Lake, I need to warn of the special language that comes along with baseball people, called "Dugout Talk." I will do my best to hold down this profanity as I've done throughout these memories thus far. Let me clarify that as I've tried to hold down! Yes, one can only try.

Every year as baseball season grew close, we'd start looking over all our baseball gear from the previous year to see what was worn out and may need to be replaced. Well, there wasn't anywhere else in the world, at least for my brothers, my friends, and myself, than Gordon Chandler's Triangle Sports Shop. It was a small building that sort of looked like a mountain cabin with its wood-log looking siding covering the exterior walls. Located just out the front gate at the corner of Inyokern road and China Lake Blvd., right in the corner of what was called the Y, across the road from the Main Gate.

Mr. Chandler, also worked on the Base by day was the father of Alan, who was a year younger than me and grew up with us all on base through the years, and a younger daughter, Carolyn. He was a somewhat tall guy, maybe six foot two or so and always had a habit of pushing his glasses up off his nose, as if they were way too big for his head and sniff at the same time! Kind of odd remembering that but I can still picture him doing it today! No later than a week before baseball season we'd be in getting fitted for something new, whatever one of us brothers absolutely needed, like maybe rubber cleats, new glove, maybe sliding pads, or a new bat. Whatever was the need, the Triangle had it or could get with a quick turnaround.

I totally remember when I, as well as all my brothers, first went into Babe Ruth or Pony League. This was the first time we were allowed to wear metal spikes! What a thrill it was to walk in metal spikes. I mean like it made us feel really cool, like the big kids, ten feet tall. I will never forget that thrilling and exciting feeling! I always remember the old timers talk about the mean ole Ty Cobb, a pro baseballer hall of famer from the old days who was known for sliding into a base "spikes-up," and if given any shit, he'd be on ya' like a bad rash, always ready for a fight. Trust me, if you ain't got scars from being spiked, well, you just didn't play a lot of baseball!

OPENING NIGHT CEREMONIES

Oh my gosh, where does one start when talking about baseball at China Lake back in the fifties and sixties. If there was any one event that drew the interest of the whole community, of all the events our parents provided for the youth of the Base, it was baseball, including all the beautiful fields and facilities. The largest of being Schoeffel field, named after a Naval officer and major player in planning the beginning of the Naval Ordnance Test Station at China Lake, Rear Admiral Malcolm Schoeffel, Deputy Chief of the Bureau Ordnance.

A beautiful grass infield with a major league dimension outfield fence with a nice and very large scoreboard in centerfield, some 420 feet from home plate. Schoeffel field, where the mighty China Lake Little League baseball season officially started each season in early June with what was called "Little Leagues Opening Night" and the parade of teams of some twenty players per team, all in matching team uniforms. Each team marched across home plate, tipping their hats, while they were introduced to the large crowd and then proceeded down the first base line, around the infield to line up next to the previous team that had just marched through.

Parade of teams, opening night ceremonies

Starting from third base line, this large group of teams would surround the large infield all the way back around to first base to the bigger Babe Ruth guys, all facing the large crowd. Crowds that I honestly would estimate every year to be around fifteen to twenty thousand local China Lake folks. The Public Works Department would have to bring in twice the number of additional bleachers to accommodate so many baseball fans. It was a night the Little Leaguers looked forward to every year.

Just after the parade and lining up of teams around the infield, then at the center of the infield just around the pitcher mound would begin the introductions starting with the president of each league, the board of directors, the military contingency, always led by the commanding officer of the Base, Ms. Little League queen, the Color Guard, and then, of course, the introduction of the Celebrity Master of Ceremonies for the evening's events.

1962 BOARD OF DIRECTORS AND DIGNITARIES.

Civilian and Military dignitaries, Little League opening night ceremonies

Every year for the little league program, with the help and coordination of the Special Service Department and the US Military support service, USO flew into China Lake by Navy jet these special celebrity guest from Hollywood or in some year's professional baseball players from the Southern California Angels.

Several of the more memorable celebrities, starting with the first that I can recall, Dale Robertson, the Hollywood TV actor from the western series called *Tales of Wells Fargo*, who came to visit China Lake little league in 1957 as the celebrity for little league's opening night ceremonies. In 1958, Will Hutchins from the TV series *Sugarfoot*, a weekly western series on ABC. In 1959, I believe Hugh O'Brian from another weekly TV series, Wyatt Earp along with his famous Butt-Line special at his hip was our celebrity guest, and in 1960 the actor Alan Hale, Jr. had a newly released motion picture called *Up-Periscope*. More known later for his role as The Skipper on *Gillian's Island's* TV series.

In 1961, the Navy flew in two California Angel Pitchers, Eli Gerba and Ryan Duran, for Opening Night. I remember Ryan Duran, the California Angels pitcher with the very thick, coke bottle like glasses. Hell-of a pitcher in those days for the Angels!

Welcoming Alan Hale to Little League opening night ceremonies

One other huge part of the evening, especially for players, was the selection of teams to play in the exhibition games that presided over all the introductions and ceremonies. Two teams from each league would be chosen by the current Miss Little League, who would pick baseballs with team names on them from each league from a box held high above her head by the Celebrity Master of Ceremonies. Then the two teams chosen from each league would square off for three innings, starting with the older little league players ten, eleven, & twelve-year-old teams in AA and A-League division and then the Babe Ruth League teams would finish off the evening. This changed a little after the 1962 season as the Babe Ruth League went away and Pony & Colt League took its place.

When the Little League queen started picking teams, this was the point of the evening all us ball players were shitten in our pants, with fingers and legs crossed for good luck in hopes to be picked to play in front of twenty thousand folks, serious! At eleven and twelve years old, such an honor for us little gamers. I remember for weeks before this special night I'd beg and plead, including an offer of a large Hershey Bar, to Miss Little League if she'd pick the Yankees.

(Miss Little League, Susan Swanson picking teams from the box of baseballs as Ryan Duran holds the box and Eli Gerba reads the teams.)

Well, maybe just jokingly to the two young beauties I remember from the 1961 and 1962 season and who both I knew well, Karen Hughes, Miss Little League in 1961, and Susan Swanson the following year, best friends then and very popular young ladies of the Base back in those early days. Believe it or not, I communicate with both these ladies still today, as we turn the corner into our seventies. Hey, what the hell, probably my first experience with bribing but I took it to the bank as my Yankees teams were picked and played in both my eleven- and twelve-year-old years for Single-A Little League games! Other Miss Little League that I recall were, 1959 Sylvia Castaneda, just before Karen and just after Susan, 1962-63 was Rita Paine, who I knew and played sports and partied with a couple of her brothers, Cliff and Eddie.

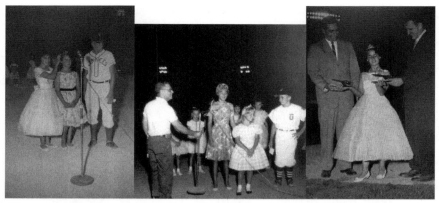

Queen Silvia crowns new queen Karen Hughes with escort Steve Metcalf.

Outgoing queen Susan crowns new queen, Rita. Bob Brown as escort.

Queen Karen presents Master of Ceremonies guest with the Navy's prestigious sidewinder missile plaques.

Little Leagues Opening Night was always such a big event for us kids of the Base, starting off our summer of fun.

4th of July was another special night for Little League's baseball program each year. It always started earlier in the day so more teams could play on this special day. Every league would have several games going on all the fields around this central area, the large Schoeffel field, the Pony field, and the two little league fields down below Kelly Field as people would walk from different fields watching youth baseball at its best. This was certainly a high point for us players, but the real high, not only for the players but the whole darn community, was once all the games were completed, the sun down and darkness came upon us, with usually a large beautiful moon coming up over "B" Mountain; all these players, their family's along with everyone else who lived on Base, came over to Murray school and on to the Burroughs Football, Kelly Field. As families, guys with their girlfriends, and many groups of friends would lay out their blankets and basket of food and drinks as parents lit and held sparklers to the amazement of their very small children. While, of course, the always mischievous of the bigger desert kids would be setting off firecrackers and running around the field with sparklers throwing them at each other and very much annoying most of the people around. Yes, if not for being with a girlfriend, peacefully enjoying the evening with my head on a comfortable lap, I too most likely would have been one of the mischievous little pricks running amuck, annoying everybody around the Kelly Field.

All this in anticipation for the China Lake Fire departments annual fireworks show they set up just across the street from Kelly Field and maybe 300 yards east across Richmond Road to the dry Mirror Lake. I mean who even named it that? Oh well, as always, the fire department put on a specular firework show that felt like fireworks were bursting just above the thousands of folks on the field, as we watched in wonder of the beautiful display of exploding colors, dancing and shooting a cross the sky in front of a large, usually full moon, over the infamous "B" Mountain. This was always a family night to be remember, as I still do some 65 years later…

Obviously by all the fun, special guests and always huge crowds, baseball's opening night is a sure indication of the importance baseball was, not only to the kids but most of the community. In the fifties and sixties, there really wasn't many competing sports for the younger kids to play, until jr. high school at Murray 7th and 8th grade where we were offered competitive flag football and basketball. We only had baseball.

My dad, Charlie, was a total baseball guy and with seven sons had damn near his own team, and from the get go, starting with my oldest brother Dave, another baseball fanatic, Charlie, of course always supported by my mom, was always involved in China Lake Little League and Babe Ruth baseball. A President of Babe Ruth, and most likely Little League one time or other, he and many of the Base higher up's, military and civilians who were all deeply involved putting this Little League program at China Lake together. They built fields; Charlie, and the others, by way of using his civil engineers construction connections and the use of public works heavy equipment and man power, impossible in today's world, to put together some pretty fine baseball fields and programs for all ages.

I'm not even sure when the huge Schoeffel field, the main baseball field on Base, was built, but obviously it was the first, not only for the locals, but for the contingency of military on Base in the early days. I do somewhat remember when the first two little league fields were built and the dedication ceremonies. They were located just a few hundred yards south of Kelly Field and east of Murray schools woodshop building. Most 7th & 8th grade boys remember Mr. McNeil's woodshop and of course his son Don (Squeaky), a well-known first China Lake family. The new little league fields Diamond # 1, closest to the woodshop, and Diamond # 2, just east of #1 and west fronting Richmond Road looking east at Mirror Lake, had both center fields butted up almost together with a dedication memorial to Jack McLaughlin and flag pole between the two at center fields. I don't remember having infield grass, although they may have in the early years plus very nice outfields with both fields having new, dark green five-foot fence around them, each field having their own snack bar behind their home plate backstop. I will always remember the pointed style pop cans plus the popular 50-50's, always my favorite that came in cherry and orange with vanilla ice-cream in the middle, also always a freebie as an award that came with returning a foul ball to the snack bar! One main distinctive difference at Diamond #2 was the 30-foot-high metal staircase leading up to the announcers and scorekeeper's booth just above the first base dugout alongside Richmond road. Gordy Irvin and Albert Hyles tell a great story about this announcer's booth. One Saturday afternoon, they were riding by the field on their bikes and saw Joe Seibold, coach of the little league Giants, up in the booth, so they snuck-up the stairs and while the door was closed, they locked the door and took off. Well, apparently the only way Joe could get out was climb out the announcers' window and climb down the chain link back stop fence. He was not happy, although the three joke about it today! Yep, Gordy & Albert again!

My Dad started us Martin boys out very early playing baseball, and thinking about it now, Charlie must had been in seventh heaven having all these boys, at least four of the first five. My older brother Steve, several years younger than Dave, really wasn't into sports except for archery of which he was very good! The other much younger two, Paul and Drew, both very good athletes themselves, came onto the seen some five and seven years after Duke (respectively). We all had quality sports ability starting at a very young age. I mean, I was shagging for Dave when I was like four or five years old. We all played baseball through the China Lake program and then most continued into high school with Dave, Duke, and I further on into college and beyond. As I remember, we started at 58-A Rowe and just behind the house, beyond the tree ditches Charlie had public works clear some desert out for us to have our own field, if that's what yeah want' a call it. Here's how I would describe our little desert field: "A no-bushes, manyrocks and holes hard pan ground as an infield and outfield. Defiantly nose bleeders and shin-burgers type ground!"Dad also had made, out of chain link fence, an eight-foot long and six foot high backstop behind home plate and a little bump for the pitcher's mound some 60'6" from the plate. We'd spend at least an hour a day when on the field picking up the larger golf ball size rocks before working out. This was usually during the weekends when my dad was able to work out with us. The rest of the summer weeks, we'd be doing our own workouts with Dave in control. Usually, Dave and I would be out in the early summer mornings, the rest of the Martin boys at different times would work out with us.

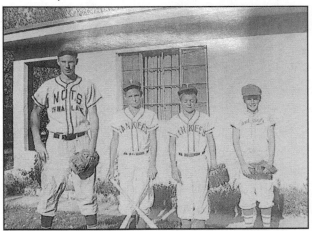

Brothers, L-R Dave, Roger, Me, and Duke.

To this day, I still remember, I mean how could I ever forget, one Saturday morning my dad had most of us out on our desert field, and he wanted to see Roger pitch from the mound and told me to get the gear on, meaning the catchers gear. "No problem Pop, I got this," not knowing shit about catching but ready to give it a try. So, I start warming Roger up while little sixth brother, Paul, and Duke were out in the outfield chasing a fucking lizard off the field. Dave jumped on their ass to get their head in the game! So with Dad standing on the side of Roger, watching his form, and I'm behind the plate screwing around with Roger, trying to make him laugh while serious Pop watches his form, putting my face behind the large catcher's glove and then poking out with some kind of dump face to make Roger crackup laughing. So as we continued for a few minutes and then one more face joke as I popped my mug out from the glove and bam! Not realizing he'd thrown the ball, I get a Roger's fastball right in between my fucking nose and my mouth! Oh, good lord did I bleed, I mean this son-of-a-bitch caught me smack in the upper lip. Just un-believable, so for the next two months I could not eat, anything going into my mouth was done through a straw. The scab that finally came was bigger than my fist, I mean a real pretty site! Dave would usually remind me weekly, "What-ya get fuckin round" (Baseball lingo for, "That is what you get for fuck-ing around.") Yeah right, for sure! I could always count on the "Rat Daddy," as us brothers nicknamed Dave to give me sound advice! RIGHT.

DODGER BLUE THROUGH AND THROUGH

Back in the early to late fifties as baseball was raging in the blood of all us kids across America, the closest professional baseball team to China Lake was the LA Angels and Hollywood Stars of the "Near Major Leagues" Pacific Coast League of California. This all changed in the spring of 1957. The National League baseball owners voted to allow the New York Giants and the Brooklyn Dodgers to move to San Francisco and Los Angeles, respectively, and in 1958 history was made as Major League Baseball opened on the west coast of the United States. Both the new Los Angeles Dodgers and San Francisco Giants were introduced to the overjoyed, west coast baseball fans as New York City fans were devastated and heartbroken.

So the Los Angeles Dodgers era began every summer evening, especially at the Martin's house at 58-A Rowe with the same wonderful voice that radi-ated from our transistor radio, "Well hello everybody, from the Los Angeles Memorial Coliseum, I'm Vince Scully along with Jerry Doggett bringing you Dodger Baseball." And, of course, three years later it was from "Beautiful Dodger Stadium." Just above downtown LA in the mountainous Chavez Rav-ine, where the brand-new home of the Dodgers opened the season in 1962.

My brother Dave was the fanatic Dodger fan of the family, followed by Roger, me, and Duke. I mean Dave so loved the Dodgers from that first season at the Coliseum in 1958. Dave, maybe his sophomore year in high school, would keep score in his store-bought scorebooks, every game the Dodgers played at home. It finally got so expensive buying scorebooks, he would make his own scoresheets with line paper, boxing in at least twelve innings in case a game would go into extra innings. When Dave couldn't make a game for some reason, which wasn't very often, he'd have Roger keep score for him and if Roger couldn't then I'd do the scoring. No shit, that's how fanatic my family was having the Dodgers 200 miles away. This score keeping continued through the three years the Dodgers were at the Coliseum and until Dave went away to San Diego State for college. Dave had collected boxes after boxes of completed Dodger game scoresheets over those three years.

Dave, a pretty darn good catcher, decided to go to college even with an opportunity to sign with the Cincinnati Reds. A good friend of my Dads, Chuck Mangle, who worked on Base in Special Services and wrote a sports blog in the Base paper, The Rocketeer, was also an associate scout for the Reds. Chuck was able to arrange for Dave to catch the Reds pre-game batting practice (BP) before all nine games the Dodgers hosted the Reds at the Coliseum in 1960. Oh my gosh! I was like twelve years old, and you can bet your ass I was there on every one of those trips. Always with my dad, Dave of course and a lot of the time Duke and/or Roger, every outing of BP Dave caught for dem Reds! I mean, we drove the four hours over the LA Crest highway and into LA to make the reds BP, maybe two hours before they'd let fans into the park. With no fans in the stands we were able to be at the wall of the front roll of seats just before the field, right by the Dodgers' dugout and maybe fifty feet from where Dave was catching BP in the cage. Can you imagine, sometimes five feet away from your hero's as they'd walk buy bullshitting with each other, playing catch, or just saying high to us little gamers and, of course, signing autographs for us. Something very special for sure!

We just hang out in the Coliseum in our great, comped seats while waiting for Dave to shower and change, and then we'd stay to watch the evenings game, certainly making the late road trip home long and dark. Oh, what a beautiful thrill it was to a twelve-year-old baseball nut from the desert of California as I reminisce back to those special years...Anyway, the Reds offered my brother Dave a no bonus contract but Dave chose to go on to college and play baseball at San Diego State.

I have to say the Rowe Street Gang of guys were all good athletics, and we played a lot together around the neighborhood, not only baseball, but we always had pickup games of either tackle or touch football or basketball, usually at the school courts. I can still clearly recall our sandlot baseball games to determine first ups, once captains and teams were picked. I'm curious if any baseball guys remember, as one captain would toss a baseball bat parallel to the other captain and where he grabs the bat with one hand would be the starting point, then the one who tossed the bat would place his hand on top of the others hand and vice-versa until they get to the knob of the bat. The captain that ends up at the knob of the bat then would grip the bat at the knob as tight as he can with one hand at the knob, holding it out from his body as the other captain would then have three tries to kick, with the side of his foot (soccer style), the bat out of the hand of the other captain. If successful, then his team gets first-up and if not, the other team is up first. Yeah, seems kind of goofy now but that's how we did it back then!

Not only from our territory, over in the Independence Street neighborhood, Teddy, Bobby, Albert, and Troy were very good baseball players and along with Herbie and Gordy from the east Independence territory, all the same good athletes and always played and participated in all the sports since little kids, all the way through high school. I'm talking about a bunch of us around the same age went through Base Little League and Pony/Colt league programs either together or half the time. This was due to the league cut off age as of the end of July, as this would make some players one-league age older depending when his birthday fell. Let's say guys my age, players like Teddy and me, our birthday's fell in August after the July deadline, making us a league age lower than lots of the guys that were the same age but birthdays fell before July 31st, making them one league age older. So when Teddy and I were league age eleven, we were playing with our peers but who were league age twelve, guys like Albert, Gordy, Herbie, Tom Kline, Metcalf, just to name a few, and when we, Teddy and I, were league age twelve and still in little league, they were up in their first years in in Babe Ruth. We were playing with league age eleven guys, like my brother Duke, Dikes, Bobby, and Mike Mead.

Then there were guys like from the Rowe Street Gang, my brother Roger, Bobby Sorge, and Rich Mead were like two league-age older and really didn't play in these leagues much with us league age younger guys. But, oh shit, did we all play together in a lot of pickup, sandlot type games in the streets or ally's around the neighborhood or at the school fields close by. It all depended on what the season that was the sport we'd play and the Rowe Street guys, as I had mentioned all very good athletes, would play these pick-up games hard and competitively. It didn't matter if it's on grass, in the dirt alleys, or in the fucking street. We played-em hard!

I must say, with all the good young talent of just baseball players around my age on Base, it must have been obvious to the little league officials that they needed to divide up this talent to make play equal by dividing up players for each league in keeping it very competitive. They knew what they were doing and did a hell of a job, as I remember my eleven and twelve year-old summer years were very competitive. One obvious rule was family members, or brothers would automatically be on the same team. I did play with Roger back in single-A due to the brother rule, even thou I was two league ages younger; the league let me play with the older guys!

One other memorable thing I will always remember, in fact, many of us ole little leaguers still reminisce about, is all the cool coaches that we had in little league, most all, fathers of their kids playing the game. This, without a doubt, made the competition between teams so much more competitive! These coaches were so into the game at least as much as the kids, if not more. Although, I must say they made sure the rules of engagement, basically, play the game hard, fair, and to the best of your ability and to win. But win or lose hold your head high and congratulate your opponent. These coaches were such a huge part of those memorable days, it just wouldn't be right not to mention, at least the ones that I can remember from my three years in Single-A little league, where it all started.

As a ten-year-old and a very young player for single-A, which was the highest age eleven & twelve league. I was invited to play and was brought up from nine & ten year old's AA-league to my brother Roger's team, the Yankees. Yep, with the big boys. (Ha Ha.)

There were a few coaches that were in their last year of coaching, as their sons would be moving up to the next age level, Babe Ruth league. The first of these coaches that comes to mine, I'm not really sure if he was the manager or coach was Clyde Zills, the father of Ronnie and Nita. Mr. Zills was a very tall, maybe 6'4" and thin. The main thing I always remember with coach Zills is he always would wear his ball hat in a fun way, tilted to the side of his head. I thought it was kind of cool!

Mr. Hogue, coach of the Pirates and his two sons, oldest, Danny a twelve year old and younger son Terry, who was league age eleven at this time. Mr. Hogue was at least 6'6" and just a mountain of a guy and as nice as can be, as were his two sons. I think both Danny and Terry grew to at least 6'5" out of high school. Terry and I were always pretty good friends and did a lot of running around together. I do have a few stories of Terry and hope I get a chance to reminisce on those stories! Mr. Jessie Bell father of Bruce and Gary coached the Red Sox, was a good friend of the kids around the Base. Bruce and I ran some together back in second through fourth grade. I remember Mr. Bell taking us to the Drive-In a few times and spending the night at their house. There was Joe Seibold who coached the Giants, Mr. Robin Fuller for my three years in the league was always coaching the Dodgers. Mr. Machowsky, Mikes dad, helped coach the Tigers, along with Mr. Ralph Pinto Sr, Herbie's dad, coached during my first two years. My Yankee coach, Mr. Runchey, was always my coach for the three years I played in single-A. Geez, talk about a completive, outspoken character Jim Runchey was! Just a great guy, very positive, motivator type guy! Single-A little league, consisting of the above six teams and its managers, was the highest-level league before advancement to the older Babe Ruth league and then later split into Pony/Colt leagues…again, I mentioned these coaches because they, to us players, were just as much a part of the game and our teams as us players. We loved these guys!

1960 L.L. All Stars
Top Row – Left to Right: Ralph Moore, Bill Eason, John Roseth, Steve Metcalf, Terry Hogue, Albert Hyles, Herbie Pinto, Tom Kliene
Bottom Row – Left to Right: Steve Troy, Tom Clow, J.C. Martin, Gary Cotton, David Luzinas, Ted Sprouse, Mike Mead, Mike Sorge

CHINA LAKE ALL-STARS

The single-A Yankees managed by the notorious Jim (Mr.) Runchey had automatically picked me since Roger was on the Yankees, even though I was league age ten they took me anyway, which would give me a final three years of little leagues single-A baseball as a Yankee. This, automatically would give the Yankees my brother Duke, a good player plus my catcher when he came up as an eleven year old!

As I mentioned this was a very competitive last two years of my little league with many good players, most were good friends and very competitive players as we competed in league against each other. The end of each summer season and after any playoffs to determent league champions the league and coaches would choose an All-Star team and its coaches. The All-Star team usually ended up coached by the league championship teams coaches and only for Little League division single-A age eleven and twelve year old.

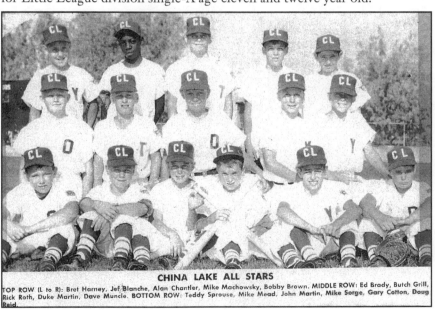

CHINA LAKE ALL STARS
TOP ROW (L to R): Bret Harney, Jef Blanche, Alan Chantler, Mike Machowsky, Bobby Brown. MIDDLE ROW: Ed Brady, Butch Grill, Rick Roth, Duke Martin, Dave Muncie. BOTTOM ROW: Teddy Sprouse, Mike Mead, John Martin, Mike Sorge, Gary Cotton, Doug Reid.

I was lucky to have made the all-star team both my eleven and twelve year old seasons. My first-year all-star team included some league age twelve buddies: Albert Hyles, Herbie Pinto, Steve Metcalf, Buddy Phillips, Terry

Hogue, Steve Troy and Tom Kline and 11-year old's like myself, Teddy
Sprouse, Mike Mead, and of course, Da' Dikes (Sorge). As you can see so many
of these guys are mention throughout these memories. As I also said earlier,
All-Stars was the only time we were able to play together until we arrived at
Burros High School baseball. We all were totally into baseball and represented
the Base very well. Oh yeah! Just to rub it in a little, without dispute, we always
beat the Ridgecrest team to advance to the next district. I'll never forget every
morning having 6 A.M. All Star practices at diamond #1 field. One morning
many of us were a little early and standing around visiting, waiting for the
coaches to show and here comes Herbie Pinto, a twelve year old driving his
dads little Volvo to practice, yes, at twelve years old! Nobody could believe it,
shit at that age no one even new how to drive, never mind a stick shift! Crazy
shit for sure! Only on the Base.

Colt League All-Star Team (1963)
Top Row: Left To Right: Manager-Giants, John Manger[66], Steve Metcalf[66], Ted Sprouse[66] Barney
Franich[66] Billy Byrd[66], Tom Clow[65], Albert Hyles[66], David Martin. Kneeling: From Left To Right: Dean
Smith[66], David Luzinas[65], Tom Hibbs[66], John Martin[66], Herbie Pinto[66], Warren Turnbaugh[65],
Buddy Phillips[65], Roy Schultz (?)[66].

All-Stars would be a continued experience for me as I advanced into first
year Pony League. This was the first year that Babe Ruth League was abol-
ished, and the new Pony/Colt league system was implemented for the main
reason of separating or splitting up the Babe Ruth's age limit. There was no
age separation between the new young thirteen year old, up from little league
with the more mature and advanced sixteen or seventeen year old. So to make
it more peer group equal at this certain age, they divided the kids into two
leagues, thirteen & fourteen year old Pony League and fifteen & sixteen year
old Colt League, defiantly a good idea especially for the new young thirteen
year old's coming out of little league.

I was fortunate to make the All-Star teams the two years in Pony League and both years in Colt League along with most of the guys (players) I played with in little league All-Stars, again, separated against each other in league but together for every end of season All-Stars.

I think it was the summer of second year Pony all-stars and Bobby Brown and I were riding his scooter with me on the back going through the desert just joy riding and hit a hole and flipped the scooter as we both went flying. I somehow cut the top of my hand at the wrist, requiring five stitches to close, yep! Right before our opening game against Bishop and I was the projected starting pitcher. I couldn't play. Oh shit was my Dad pissed at me as he told me more than once, he didn't want me riding on any motorcycle.

My first post season all-star year as a fifteen year old colt leaguer was with a pretty memorable team, including that years coaching staff, the manager, a new and young Navy Lieutenant Bill Borkstad, and my brother Dave, both in their early twenties, experienced baseball guys and very good with us older colt/high school players. The league officials had the Colt League All-Star team that year wear NOTS China Lake uniforms to represent the Base as the team participated in post season. This team included many of the guys I played All-Stars with back in little league as you should recognize some of the names, guys who I can remember like Steve Metcalf, Teddy, Herbie, Albert, Buddy Phillips, Bill Byrd, Barney Franish, Tom Clow, Warren Turnbaugh, and new comer John Manger.

Over all those years that I was in All-Stars and the years following as I remember, the China Lake baseball All-star teams always won the early district tournaments and usually the second rounds covering the high desert area of Southern California up to Bishop and down to around the Barstow, Palmdale/Victorville areas. Most always losing as we advanced into District 3 competition, usually down in the LA, Southern California areas! These same players, at least most since we were eleven year old little leaguers are the same guys I went through four years of Burros High School baseball with together. All in All, just a great and wonderful experience with guys that even today I still have great friendships, and who I still visit and vacation with together.

In speaking for all us little leaguers throughout those first years of baseball on Base, my personal thanks to my dad, Charlie, Mom and all the snack bar ladies, all the Little League, Babe Ruth and Pony/Colt league directors, coaches, staff, and so many parent supporters throughout those wonderful years back in the fifties and sixties, those exciting times of Little League baseball there on Base at China Lake.

I would like to add a personal and sentimental note to end these wonderful memories from the early days of China Lake baseball, just to emphasize how much of an impact so many years since these memories had on me!

Charlie, my dad, passed away in 1999 and as I held his hand that last day, after some other very meaningful words, I whispered softly in his ear and thanked him for the beautiful childhood life he gave all of us, especially those great family days and all those games of China Lake Little league, the wonderful Opening Day ceremonies. "You were always out there with us each year, always trying to make it better! Thanks for the memories! I could not have asked any more from a Father." Yep, this is what he heard as he took his last breath…

"Rock in Fire" Charlie….

CHAPTER 7
Places In Common

FRONT AND BACK GATES

How fortuitous it is to bring back my memory search of places that all who grew up on Base, back in the old days that we had in common to enjoy, or in this case, patiently, endeared. I think I'd better set the stage. I mean, if one hasn't experienced living on a military base, as I'm sure most have not, I'd like for you to think back to where you actually did grow up. Maybe a town, a city, wherever it may have been, we'll just call it your community. Think about this, what if you had to have a pass or ID always on your person and had to show this pass to an armed and uniformed military security guard at an entrance gate to your community, before you were allowed to enter your community to go home? I'm probably making it sound more like a prison or concentration camp, right? Well, it really wasn't bad as it may seem, as we grew-up in this environment it just became part of our lives. We just had to learn quicker than most, at a very much younger age, basically, to carry an ID. "Don't forget your Base pass" the last words we'd usually hear heading out the door. I personally lived this way for my first eighteen years of life, as all my family members and so many friends growing up at this same time on Base. This pass also was required going to the movies, pools, gym, the Exchange and commissary, any and all military facilities on Base.

I will always remember in the early days back in the fifties, back when at least two Marines always in full dress uniforms, were on post, not only the main front gate but the back gate on Richmond Road. Going back as far as I can remember, driving with my parents or a friend's parents when going off Base and returning, all personal in the vehicle were required to show their pass, although, except for the driver. If any kids had forgot their pass, the guard would most likely salute you through. I also can remember thinking it was so cool going through the front gate with friends whose dad was a Naval officer. Now all the military officers usually had an officer's sticker on the windshield, where no stopping to show a pass was required. If the officer was in another vehicle that may not have an officers sticker and his military ID was required, in either the case, the sharp dressed Marine would "Snap Too" attention and salute, kicking his heals together as his white gloved hand and blue sleeve would tightly move to his white peaked capin response to the officers sticker or ID. This was just so awesome; it would actually bring goose bumps up and down my arms! I mean like serious military shit...

As far back as we can remember, society has lived by rules and laws. Law, of course, is a set of legal rules designed to help keep order, protect property, and keep people safe. Rules are basically a set of instructions to help people live and work together. The biggest difference, I suppose, would be the consequences! Those of us who lived and grew up on Base certainly respected and obeyed the rules and laws of America's society, no problem! Different from regular society, we also had a few military rules to adhere to. There was one rule the military made sure all, including kids, respected and obeyed, that I'm positive everyone growing up on Base, since its inception, will never forget. It was a rule designed as a continued reminder for the good folks working and living at this secret city. Always there in plain sight, bolded in red and black letters on a large 4'x6' sign, set up to be very visible from your car as you entered or exited the Base front gate from each side of the road. The message was clear and precise. It's what I referred to as "The Here Rule." I'll let the smaller version of the sign in the photo below (most likely from the back or high school gate) illustrate this special military rule to REMEMBER:

There was one incident way back in either the late fifties or early sixties that everybody should remember and if not, well, this certainly should restore your memory! It happened one early morning, say around 2 A.M. out at the back gate, where, at that time of night, there would be very minable to no traffic at this very dark, desolate Base back gate. As I remember from all the news and rumors was that apparently, two Marines, bored and with nothing much to do, decided to have a "Quick Draw" contest with their chamber cleared revolvers. Well, it turned out one of the guns was not chamber free, and as they drew, one of the Marines shot and killed the other Marine! This was, for our small community, a huge event and was the talk of the Base. But, you know, I just don't remember us civilians hearing much more about the incident, or just maybe, I don't remember any more than I'm stating. OKAY, Okay, I know, that makes more since! Right...fine! But here's my theory. So if you know anything about the military, you'd know how they work very hard keeping this type of shit or incident out of the press, military only, or basically, "Need to know." End of story. As far as I know, that's all I ever heard, that's all I ever knew...OKAY? ... Who-raw!

Base Theater

The base theater is the large square building

The base theater was much more than just a movie house, it also had a large stage for the performing arts. Located perfectly in the center of the base in Bennington Plaza, the theater had just one screen and was one of the most active meeting places for us kids. I can't recall the exact time frame; I'd guess we must have been around seven or eight years old when we were able to go to the "Show" without an adult. What I do remember back then is that we were allowed to walk from our territory on Rowe Street all the way to the Base theater, which seemed so far for us young guys. I also very much remember when we first started going to the movie show that it only cost ten cents, which would give us a "color cartoon," the "newsreel," the news of the world, and a "short" (a continued episodes maybe five minutes long of some kind of short series) all this prior to the main movie.

OH YEAH, one other thing most important was before any showing was all movie goers in the theater would stand for the national anthem. Wouldn't it be interesting to know if other theaters outside of the Base, across the country, actually had the national anthem played before every movie, or was it customary just on a Military base. I would have to believe everyone would stand for the anthem back then as there was so much patriotism throughout the country during this early post war time. Again, just curious! Our earliest ventures to "The Show," as I said, we'd usually walk unless we'd get lucky and one of our parents would drop us off. We'd have to start out at least an hour before show time and would have to walk through a few other neighborhood territories on the way. During the summer, this was at least a once a week occurrence, most always the 1:00 P.M. Saturday matinée. At this age, we were pretty good kids and ,let's say, less mischievous when we were inside the theater as we were most of the time outside on the way home.

On our way home, we would usually play out the movie we had just watched. As an example, let's say the main show on a particular afternoon was *The Adventures of Zorro*, you remember that sword fighting, black mask and cape hero with his black horse and always helping the poor folks in Mexico from the devious sheriff. So on our walk back home, we all would brake branches off trees to use as our sword and we would sword fight all the way home. Say if the movie was a cowboy and Indians western movie, then of course we'd play like cowboys and Indians as we shot-em up all the way home. Yep, just kids letting our imagination run wild. As we got older and so much more mischievous and adventurous, about the time we started looking and thinking of girls, maybe thirteen or so, well, the theater became much more than what the hell was showing on the screen. A time when the Saturday matinee was now for the little kids and us bigger kids started going to the movies at night, and of course there was *American Bandstand* on television every Saturday around 12:30 early afternoon. Man! We just couldn't miss Dick Clark and his American bandstand! Right?

Usually, the girls would go in their little group and the guys would be in their group. The theater seats were aligned in three sections, from the west, right side aisles and around 15 or so seats in each row, a larger center rows with maybe 25 seats in each roll and a left, east side with the same seating as the west side. Us young kids, girls and the boys, would always set about one-third the way down on the west, right side rows of seats. If the word was out a girl liked a certain guy, well this was the place he'd meet up with her and they would set together. Of course the girl always had her girlfriends on the other side of her and as always, giggling about what ever stupid thing they'd be whispering about! The guy would always have his buddies sitting just behind him and egging him on and joking about him getting a fill. I do remember numerous times of me in this situation and my buddies sitting behind me with their never-ending encouragements, as it would take at least ten minutes into the main movie to get my arm up and around the back of her seat, only to hear the stupid giggling just behind us! "He's filling her up" or "he's getting some now." Totally irresponsible little pricks, as if I didn't do the same thing to them in the same situation, ha-ha-ha! We would had probably shit our pants if we actually were able the cop-a-feel, as little as they'd have been at that age, and of course as I think about it, I'm only describing the guys side and what was the only thing on our minds at that age, from the girls standpoint I'm guessing it was more a popularity thing and just "boy crazy stuff." I'm sure or at least believe at that age the girls didn't go to the movies in hopes of getting their little tit's mauled by this new crazy crush! Ha-Ha...no, they needed a few more years!

I remember always feeling bad or, I guess, more embarrassed for Barbara Roberts, Karen Marker's aunt (same age, just Karen's mother is Barbara's sister) when almost every time Barbara was at the movies, as we all set around each other in that west side seat area, her mother would come down the aisles with a flashlight looking for Barbara to make sure, at least I assume, that Barbara wasn't there with a guy. I'm not talking just a few times, I'm talking about many times for several years! Like I said I felt bad for her! Now, Barbara and I get a good laugh over that today...

Being mischievous in the movies was always so easy for the Rowe Street Gang, like moving over to the middle rolls of seats where we could finger flick popcorn into the movie projection lights, creating like shooting stars into the foggy night and of course irritating all the adults sitting around us. As you see, I mentioned "foggy" because back in those days' adults could smoke in the theater and many of them did. Matter of fact, the theater supplied ashtrays in the seats armrest! So, let's just say, we were just irritating them back! Right? We did get kicked out of the theater a few times for flicking popcorn. I also remember Bobby (Sorge) one time bringing with us a throwing dart and for an hour dared each other to throw it into the movie screen during the show. A scary deed for sure at our age but finally Bobby got up the nerve and from the middle seats stood up and threw the dart into the screen. Well, with the lights out and the movie showing you couldn't see the dart unless you really looked hard. Oh yeah, it was there and it stayed in that movie screen for years to come. I'm willing to bet if that screen hasn't been replaced or the dart found, it should still be there.

Movie shows weren't the only entertainment the theater offered. With its big stage the schools used it for plays, singing performances, and during

Christmas time the Base had Santa Clause events for the base kids. The biggest event I will never forget, as I'm sure all those who also were there feel the same. That special evening in the late sixties when special services brought in the Beach Boys for a one-night concert. This was just at the time "Surfer Girl" and "Little Duce Coup" were like one & two on the billboard charts. Just a great night of listing and dancing to the Beach Boys at our own Base theater. They made a point to say no dancing but ten minutes into the music we were all up and dancing in the aisles. I was so lucky that night as the beautiful Sally Burum, a lifelong friend, and I hooked up just as the dancing begin and we danced together to the Beach Boys the whole damn concert! What a thrill. I also heard from those who were there much later that night, after the concert, each of the Beach Boys had drove his own car up from Hawthorn California, all Corvettes and later that night were drag racing some of the locals up on Trona Road. Hmm, liked to have been there for that event. Anyway, certainly, a night to remember at "The Base Theater"!

Front entrance of the Station Theater in July 1949.

I don't really ever remember going out town to Ridgecrest to the Ridge Theater, especially when we were younger but I sure remember going to the Crest Drive-in (The Crest)! Located just outside the front gate and west on Inyokern road a few miles, as kids we'd go with our parents or other friends' parents. Back in those days the drive-In theaters were very popular across the country, and we felt very special to have one so close to us on Base! As we grew older and into high school, well, that was a much different experience. Friday and Saturday nights were the main two nights when we would usually make our presents at the Crest and in one or two ways. First, if you had a special girl or maybe a date, then you were ear marked for at least one night with her and a nice relaxing evening with a good movie, popcorn, drink and a comfortable companion...OR, three or four of us would go with one of the guys who had a car or his parents' car, most likely several of us hidden in the trunk along with booze we were to indulge that evening.

Once in we'd usually find some other friends we would park next too and just kind of make a party of it. As I recall, Big Mike, the owner of not only the drive-in but the Ridge Theater also, was pretty cool about what he would see, mainly he just didn't want any loud talking and partying during the show. Basically, show respect to the other movie go'ers. We sure had a lot of fun out there at the ole Crest Drive-In. It was really one of the big and very popular thing to do for the teenagers in the valley back then!

THE OFFICERS CLUB AND OTHER POOLS

Here's one for you to think about! Some twenty-five thousand plus people living in California's Mojave Desert together in a small, say ten mile square, community and where during the summer months the temperature can rise above the 120 degree mark with a consistent average of around 110 degrees. I mean "HOT" tamales to say the least! Now keep in mind, not a house on the Base had a swimming pool, except maybe a little plastic kid baby pool or the old slip & slide's. No shit we used to get one every summer and had a ball practicing our baseball hook slides, running, and diving to slide down to the other end. Okay, but that's all we personally had. I recall way back at the beginning in the mid-fifties or so my parents would take us out to the Navy's Armitage Field and across the large parking lot, just pass the big hangers to what I believe we called "The NAF Pool."

As a very young kid, I so remember the pool parking lot was made from: Remember those old large, steel portable aircraft runway landing tracks with probably 80 percent cut out with holes, maybe five feet wide by eight feet long? I'm sure made and used for the SEABEES portable aircraft landing runways on islands in the Pacific during the war. It was so damn hot in the summer, there's no way to walk on that steel without shoes, even then you could feel the heat. I don't think that pool lasted long or at least we never went back out there as we grew older.

The only other swimming pools on Base included the Base indoor pool, located in the same building complex next to the base gym in the Center Plaza. I actually hung out in this sports facility, the gym & pool quite often, starting around 7th grade. I guess I was what you'd called a "gym rat" as I was always playing pick-up basketball games, just shooting around working on my game or in the weight room, mainly on weekends and holidays in the winter time and even more so in the summer. I mean if we weren't on the baseball field, we were in the gym. These early teen days is when I started with the weights, and all through my teen years was kind of bulking on the weights or playing hoops!

Besides myself many of my friends you may recognize were gym rats like me, besides most of the Rowe Street Gang, including my much taller brothers, Roger and Duke. Also, guys like Gordy, Teddy, Tom Chapman Tom Kleine and Ridgecrest guys Scott Shacklett, Jimmy and Johnny Ayres, Tommy Mather and always some of the much older gym rats like Chino Jacobs, Dennis Hendon, and Teddy Lane. ALL hoop guys from Burros basketball through many years! I even remember a very special few weekends in the winter, like around Christmas holiday's when I was maybe a senior in high school, like 1966 at the Burros in Ridgecrest gym. The Basketball coaches would open the gym for "hoop nuts" to work out and play pick-up games.

These two weekends I so remember was because Big Jay Carty, maybe six feet eleven inches tall, older Burros player from the very early days at Burros, was in town visiting his parents. I believe Jay actually played in the NBA with the Lakers and was currently working for the UCLA Bruins as an assistant under John Wooden for the main purpose of working out and toughing-up a Bruin Player named Lew Alcindor, AKA, Kareem Abdul-Jabbar. Anyway, the first pick-up game, five on five shirts vs skins, of course, and I was on the opposite team from the big guy and I even ended up guarding him quite a bit. Now, I'm not a big guy, maybe six foot back then, but I could play pretty good defense, especially positioning and blocking out! Well, I fought for position a little quicker that **the** big guy, what I called him as he called me "The Little Guy," as I block him out a few times. We actually had fun working each other for position, and I even think he gave me a little respect, as the second game and a week later during picking teams he would pick me, the "Little Guy," on his team! Just some hoops I remember well.

I just loved going to the gym, meeting lots of my friends for pick-up basketball games. A big part of my teenage sports life growing up for sure!

Anyhow, back to swimming pools. I got a little sidetracked with my hoop stories, huh! Next door through the gym locker room was the very large Base indoor pool with its fifteen-foot high dive and long swimming lanes. Roger and I liked going there for the high dive. We got pretty good on that board with our one and a half, two's, and even two-and-a-half front flip and Roger with a great backwards one and two tumble Gainers. Yes, there also was plenty of gawking (girl watching) there at that ole indoor pool!

There is one memorable let's call it an adventure that happened to me on one occasion while at the indoor pool by myself after playing hours of pick-up basketball next door at the gym. Well, sort of by myself. This personal experience that happened to me, some time or other happens to all young boys around the age of thirteen to fifteen. Some earlier than others and some just late bloomers as they come into puberty. Yep, that's right this young desert dawgs first, what the scientist call, an orgasm! Let's just back up, quit laughing, and let me tell my story for Christ sakes! I mean it was all pretty innocent but a very memorable part of my life.

Anyway, it was later in the afternoon, maybe around three o'clock or so, and I was in the pool with a girl a few years older than me that I knew from around the Base. I will keep her name out of this to protect the insane (Ha-ha), but she was very pretty and developed very well for her age. There were maybe a few people down on the shallow end and she and I were around the middle, in about chest high water playing grab ass with each other when she took my hand and pulled me close. Then slowly drew it down between her legs, I mean to a place I've never been before! No, I can't count the 5th grade crazy shit. An unbelievably sweet, wet feel and honestly the only thing nasty we did in the pool that day. I guess I could describe more in detail of my sensational feelings at the time, but hey, this isn't some kind of romance novel for Christ sakes! Ha-Ha. I finally got home, most likely trying to hide bulging pants, as I will never forget that continuous, unbelievable and sensational feeling that was running through my body, especially down around the ole big guy, just ready to "blast off" or explode kind of feeling. "Mom, I'm gone-a take a little nap before dinner" as I headed off to the bedroom, locking the door behind me. That's right, bunk bed and all, the most exciting and most memorable "pure feeling" I had ever experienced, at least until I got laid for the first time. Ha Ha. Yep, tough to forget that little venture as I'm sure most guys remember their first! Just another memorable summer day to remember at the ole Base! Ha Ha Ha. We're reminiscing, right?

Just a block south of the gym & indoor pool facility there was another pool, the chief petty officers pool & club (CPO) and only CPO rank families and guess were able to belong or enter. I don't ever remember swimming there, maybe hung around the fence talking to friends. I did later in life, lifeguarded for some kid's birthday party. Many of my friends from school, parents retired or former Navy enlisted, and Club members hung out at the CPO pool. I do remember many loud party's going on by them chief's over at the CPO club as we played baseball on the fields close by or walking home from the movies. They did get rowdy there at the CPO. Actually, the place burnt down I believe in the sixties but not sure if it was from the partying or what, but it burnt down. Now with that said, I must add with a little humor that the China Lake fire department is just across the street, maybe fifty yards from the CPO club! Hmm....

Grand Opening of O' Club Pool, September 24th, 1950

Then there is the notorious and prestigious Officers Club (O Club) and all its beautifully, manicured surrounding grounds located at the far east end of Blandy Avenue. Just as you enter the Hill community nicknamed "Snob Hill."

If it sounds like I might be a little bias by the start of this first description, well I certainly am! Oh my god, where does one start when writing about a place they grew up frequently visiting, every summer since we were just babies. As baby kids, through jr. high, and on into high school teenage years and beyond. Since I can remember, when we were very young, every summer Mom would bring her crew to the O Club pool for swimming. I can actually remember, although spotty, swimming in the baby's pool over by the women's dressing room, and Mom putting baby oil on us as the only sun protection back in those early days, not to say it did any good, but it really didn't matter because all Moms kids were usually very dark brown from living in the sun and desert, usually shirtless, the boys anyway. My best times at the O Club was around the jr. high, say thirteen or fourteen-year-old time frame and on after, through my teens.

This is where, from the Rowe Street Gang, Roger, me, and Duke with Dikes, Bobby Sorge, and Jimmy Nicol's all hung out during the summer unless we had a ballgame that night, then we'd try and stay away from the club or at least from swimming out in the sun. Other friends and regulars of the O Club from other neighborhoods in those early days, before we moved to the Capehart-A's, was of course Metcalf, Tom Kline, and Tom Chapman, a good friend from all the hoops we played together for so many years. Hell, I can go on and on and I haven't even mentioned the girls yet, which, in themselves, are deserving of their own beautiful memories and stories! Hey, maybe a good title, say "The O Club Girls" or "The Girls of the O Club." Hell, I can go back even earlier than jr. high to remember some of the older, brother Dave's age, girls that hung out at the O Club. Geez, beautiful but nothing like our age girls, I'm talking between say thirteen/fourteen on up to seventeen and eighteen years old, starting around the 1960's time period. To this day us guys who hung at the O Club still talk and reminisce about these special ladies of the officer's club pool. We had actual arguments of who had the darkest and perfect tan, who looked the hottest in their bathing suits, and most important, who had the nicest ass amongst our lovelies of the O Club. So okay, just to wet your whistle, although it was very close with many of these finest it was Susan Perry who got the nod for darkest & best tan vote. Just ask Chapman! This was one of the big deals both the guys and girls of our age group were very much into, getting tan.

I must mention, not only did us kids enjoy our games and daily summer fun at the O Club, but many of the officer's wives, mothers, and lady members of the Officers Club had their little day time get togethers, either down inside the main club rooms, outside on the Lani, or up by the pool. I always remember the Ladies Bridge Club would set up their weekly bridge luncheon many times, during those hot summer months outside under the long canopy covered set of nice pool tables running the length of the north side of the main pool, kind of an adult area of umbrellaed tables where they'd occupied anywhere up to ten tables for their bridge outings. Of course, booze could and would be served and these ladies certainly took advantage of a totty or two, creating some mighty fun times for these adult lovelies, at least from our observation! I actually believe the game of bridge was indigenous to military life, maybe even part of the Women's Auxiliary of the Commissioned Officers Mess (WACOM). I'm just not sure about some of the military stuff, but at least it was popular for the military and civilian folk's at China lake. I know my Mom and her sister, my Aunt Betty, were members of the Bridge club for years, and from what I understand, Aunt Betty was a masterpoints type player and traveled to many tournaments in her heydays! I remember many teenagers even played Bridge around the O Club, including my brother Roger, who with a few of our friends, mostly military or high raking dependents, would get a game going on occasion.

The O Club also had a great springboard that a lot of us dare devils competed for bragging rights for the best flips, both front and back flips. I remember Roger, who was very good on the spring board, was trying a gainer, basically as you leave the diving board straight-up and out, in mid-air, begin the back flip, a very hard back-flip to do. Anyway, Roger didn't get out far enough in starting his back flip and hit the back of his head on the diving board. Well, both lifeguards, one a guy and the other a girl, both older high school kids. The female lifeguard, a very pretty gal, was a song leader and member of the homecoming court her senior year and a real cutie. Well, the two lifeguards got Roger out of the pool and patched the small cut on the back of his head. He was fine except for a little blood, headache, and some embarrassment. Of course, the only thing he said to me was, "I can't believe it, I saw her whole tit," talking about the female lifeguard as she worked on him.

One other thing all the teens, both boys & girls that hung at the O Club back then, would remember was the ping-pong table and the old juke box attached to the wall next to the ping-pong table, all under a large wood roof style canopy covering a good 1,500 sq. ft. of concrete floor for, a fun in the shade play area leading to a well provided snack bar, which including great fries and milkshakes. A good spot for some more reminiscing! I remember in the evenings and the snack bar is closed for the day by way of dropping the large four-foot by eight-foot plywood doors down over the front window of the place and then latched from the inside. It was so easy to slip a screwdriver under the plywood to unlatch the door lock. We were able to hold it open far enough for a guy to slip halfway in, just far enough to put his mouth under the beer tap for some freebie beer! Yep, guys back then just couldn't let a few free beers go by.

Playing ping-pong every day resulted in lots of good players, creating many little tournaments and very competitive games with, of course, that ole time wall juke box blaring loudly throughout the O-Club complex and for miles around blaring all the current, what we call today "oldies but goodies" music. Songs I remember like the Beach Boys who came on the seen from southern California in the very early sixties with "Surfing USA." I can still hear songs like the Righteous Brothers' "You've lost that loving feeling," The Everly Brothers' "Cathy's Clown," The Four Seasons' "Sherry," or "Walk Like A Man" blaring all afternoon. There was more slower, romantic music come evening and into the night while flirting around with your best girl in the grass around the pool as the music continued through the warm, cool summer air, lovie-dove songs like The Danleers' "One Summer Night," Bobby Hatfield's "Unchained Melody," or Bobby Vinton's "Roses Are Red" to name a few and would usually get the couples all hot and bothered and ready for some "boy-girl" smooching.

During the summer days at the Officer Club pool was also where all the events for that summer night were planned out and usually included both the guys and girls. Either someone's parents were out of town or maybe it was time for a desert party, which in fact was where I'd say 80 percent of parties were held with both Base kids and Ridgecrest kids especially during our high school years. The desert parties as a whole were well known and remembered only that "there was a desert party last night" and that's about it as it was really hard to remember much that happen at a particular desert party night due to the overindulgence of the refreshments, at least my experience! But for sure, The desert parties throughout our teenage years and much further beyond were a huge part of all the kids' lives while growing up, not only on Base but throughout the valley.

The O Club also sponsored dances for the high school age kids during the summer nights. Most of these dances were more beach or pool dress, nice shorts and shirts, but a few were more formal, like with a coat and tie and held down on the Lani, the large canopied stage and large dance and dining area, specially designed for romantic summer desert nights under the billons of stars, close to the Barefoot Bar. All this just below the manicured lush grass that just hours earlier laid all the O Club beauties tanning to get their bod's ready for their romantic evening. Oh my, did they do that so successfully well! The Officers Club every year also hosted Grad Night, an all-night party for all seniors graduating from Burroughs High School, a big event every year for the graduating seniors and their parents, as many were at Grad Night for a few hours chaperoning or joining their grad in this huge event in their family's life. Just wonderful memories there at the O Club both when we were little kids and more importantly, through our teen years and beyond.

THE ALL-FAITH CHAPEL

Every Christmas and Easter, the boys in our family all got new shirts, but even more, I'll always remember my sisters, Marion and Liz, with their bright new dresses with handbags to match in celebration of these special days. All the family baptisms, first communions, and confirmations were held right there at the All-Faith Chapel. I remember the highly respected Catholic couple and good friends with my parents, John and Deloris DiPol were my confirmation parents. Always the subject of conversation with them when visiting in passing for so many years since. As I have mentioned, my mom being a devout catholic, these events were my mom's whole life and she made sure her Little Angels were dressed appropriate for each occasion. Yep, Dad took care of the sporting activities for the family, with Mom's support, and Mom made sure her family went to church every Sunday, holy days, and for all her sons to be altar boys. The Church values always the number one family priority.

The All-Faith Chapel was much more significant to my family that just being our church of worship. I very much remember this church facility being constructed back in the late fifties. My dad, Charlie, was one of the civil engineers in the Construction and Design Department and was always out on the new chapel construction site and on occasion would take some of us family members with him. He also had an old movie camera with him to film some of the construction. I will always remember one trip to the work site the contractor's (Drennan Construction Company out of Bakersfield) superintendent, a guy named Buck Johnson and his crew were using this huge crane in hooking up steel cables to all four sides of each large rectangular, light green concrete roof panels and placing them on the new chapel roof frame one at a time. Us kids got a big thrill when Buck Johnson would ride a few of the panels up high on to the roof. For sure a certain No-No in today's world but remember, we're talking the fifties. Oh shit, would OSHA have had a field day with that!

I also remember watching this same scene but on movie film many years later from my dad's film collection. Well, not only the construction films but so many other home movies' my parents took over the years at the All-Faith Chapel, especially of family members baptisms, first communion, conformations, or other special events. I remember the first little Catholic church we went to on Base for several years was just across Blandy Avenue from the Enlisted Men's Club (EM-Club). This small little building called chapel could probably hold a couple hundred church goers at one time and once the All-Faith Chapel was built the church was turned into the first credit union to arrive on Base.

First church on base.

I do remember all us older brothers, Dave on down to Duke, serving Mass way back then in the late fifties, black & white Cassock's and in Latin. Yep, everyone of Moms angels served Mass for at least six years. Now if you were a Catholic at China Lake in the late fifties, you would have no problem remembering Father Pointek and Monsignor Ryan, two of the most eccentric Catholic priests you'd ever want-a meet. I mean try serving Mass as an altar boy with either one of these padres. I can't believe how well I bluffed my way through without getting my ass chewed, especially the Latin part. Oh Lord, just don't try bluffing your way through confession, especially as an altar boy because they knew who you were and the ole "bless me father for I have sinned, UGH, I said a nasty word five times, I hit my brother twice," just didn't get it. But then it was hard to be honest with all the, let's say mischievous crap Roger and I did. I mean these priests wouldn't hesitate coming right out of their little confessional room and yank you right off your begging knees. Geez, talk about being embarrassed! I mean real bully stuff!

Once the All-Faith Chapel opened as we were a bit older, the Cassock's changed from black and white to Red and white and mass had changed from Latin to English, YEAH! Roger and I felt so grown up, we started helping ourselves to the wine, making sure it was ready for the priest during Mass. It tastes kind of crappy, but we still indulged. We also, on occasion, helped ourselves to the collection, kind of our own way of paying ourselves for our services as altar boys! That's right, "Mom's Little Angels." Trust me as I talk about it now, the good church has been repaid a thousand times over because of our guilty just deeds! You know, I just don't get it back then; I mean we were brought up by very proper, church going folks who taught right from wrong. We weren't rebelling against anything really! I guess I'm going to stick with "isolated little, desert rat rebels".

Hmm, this is probably a good time to mention that my parents were very much disciplinarians with their ten kids, and us kids had very much respect and love for them. Yes, as a stay at home mother, as most mothers were back in those days, she believed everything her little angels said and was so patient and understanding, but when she did get pissed, which wasn't very often, usually when one of us boys would just be so fricking defiant, well then she'd head out into the yard, right to one of the tall, thin trees with great little skinny branches that stripped of its leaves made for a perfect switch. Really shitty in the summer when wearing shorts! I guess as I think back and not knowing how bad Dave or Steve were when younger, Roger and I were probably the reciprocates of most of the switches. But of course, Roger and I both had our own way of getting, let's say, a lesser whooping than we had coming. We both knew it hurt mom as much as it hurt us, to switch one of her little angels, and when she started swinging with one hand and holding my arm with the other, starting from the get-go, I would keep flinching and bending my legs forward and crying and yelling "Ow Ow Ow"! She maybe got me with several good whacks but none really hurting too bad, but the way I was yelling you'd think I was getting switched with a wet whip or something! Once done and mom gone, it was hard not to laugh, knowing I just got away from a close call. Roger and I, reminiscing with Mom and Dad years later as adult parents over cocktails, had a very good laugh with stories like this! Really, I have to say, the best parents one could ever have, and I thank them often for a great childhood. RIP my parents.

I remember telling my Mom as a young boy, "I'm really trying to be good, but it's hard." I know that the worst thing about being an aggressive rebel was hurting and disappointing my parents! I am so thankful she only found out maybe a tenth of the shit we pulled, mainly Roger and me. In my parent's defense, having ten kids was a lot more to pay attention too. Well OKAY, how about just one more story for ole time's sake? Ha Ha. Hmm… I remember one Friday night in high school in like 1964, Roger, a junior in high school and one of his running buddies, I think Bob Barney, had my mom's car out for a Friday night school event and decided to head down to Newport Beach for the weekend, without asking. Yep, remember, this was Friday night. Well come Sunday morning as Mom planning for early Mass went out to her car and it wasn't there! Roger had it the whole weekend in Newport Beach, I mean, and this is the first time the car and Roger were noticed missing! Just an example of "hard to pay attention" to all the kids all the time. Unless you've walked in those shoes, you just wouldn't understand, as I make a sign of the cross in thoughts of my Mom! Yep, one of her "Little Angels" at it again.

(A new All-Faith chapel being constructed)

SANDQUIST SPA

The Sandquist Spa back in the early days was kind of a large picnic type area with a lot of concrete walks and grounds, almost like a huge skating rink with four-foot wood fences and attached benches, separating different picnic areas from others with a very large roller-skating rink in the middle. Located at the far west side of the Base and out toward where the Navy's Snort Rocket Slide testing facility was located. I have to believe the spa was on Base land in those early years but later annexed back to the county. The reason I say that is because in the seventies we used to have what we'd call "Cage" parties for the young city of Ridge-crest folks, including a few bands to supply the music. To get there just go out Inyokern road a few miles and head out north on a dirt road for two or three miles to the Sandquist Spa. I remember in the early days, we were fairly young and would go out, as a family to the spa for my Dads office BBQ's and some Church functions. The main thing I remember back in the old days, and thank god for, was the huge shade trees that shaded us from some of the 115 degree heat! OH! But I sure do remember the cage parties…oh Lordy!! as I was one of the organizers of a few those cage parties. Man, did we go through the beer!!

MIRROR LAKE

I'd be curious if during the Navy's recruitment advertisements, brochures, and other sales material used in the recruitment of personal for the start-up of their new California Test & Evaluation Base in the Desert of California back in the early 1940's they ever used a Lake, as in body of water to draw people's attention to this wonderful opportunity. If so and indeed used Mirror "Dry" Lake as the actual lake, well I call foul and false advertising! If there has ever been more than two inches deep of water in Mirror lake it certainly hasn't been in my lifetime which takes us back to 1948! Very seldom is there ever any water in Mirror Lake and when we do get some, it's usually in the winter from a prolong rain or snowstorm. never will it get deeper than even two inches and will stay wet for several weeks before it dries up until the next rain. There is a little history about the lake from what I've heard and understand, and that is during a rain while the water is still there a prehistoric fish called fairy shrimp that come out of the hard ground and brought to life by the water.

I have seen some recreation out on the dry lake, such as parasailing. I even have a great photo of someone doing exactly that on the dry lake.

A rare photo of Mirror Lake with water

One of the biggest events on Base each Fourth of July back in the old days was held out on the dry lake when the Base fire department presented its fireworks display in front of thousands of folks watching from the grass on Kelly

Field across the Richmond road. Also, I do remember one time I was along in my parents' station wagon after Sunday church one winter morning and after a recent rain, so there was water in the lake but was frozen solid. Now this took some time in building up the nerve but finally getting the nerve, I took off going about 30 miles an hour right into the ice covered water, and once on the ice, I pushed hard on the brake and cranked the wheel with a hard left turn as the car was completely on its own as I slid across the ice spinning like a top in very fast circles for maybe a half mile or so! Oh my gosh, what a rush that was as I really felt like I left my heart back on dry land! Once I got the car back on dry land, I went back and did the same thing a second time, only this time cranked the wheel to the right. Now, I'm not all crazy, as there was a reason behind my madness, as I wanted to get the feel, knowledge and experience in case I ever get into a car spin while on the highway I'll know what to expect, not panic and learn how to work a spin! Does that make sense?

TELEVISION

I can so easily remember, as I'm sure will so many others, climbing up on our roof, usually by shimming up the TV antenna or by ladder to adjust the antenna, as someone in the house yells out the window or door checking how the reception on the TV is looking as I slowly turn the antenna, carefully not to wind the TV wires too tight until the yell from below comes, "Great, right there." Yep, this was a time around the mid-fifties and TV was pretty new to us all on Base. Our TV was pretty typical as with most folks on Base, a three-foot by three-foot box that's set up on four, three-inch legs. On top of the TV was what we called a "rabbit ears" type antenna and wires connecting at the back of the box to the TV tube located inside the box, all running out the window and on up the antenna pole which was attached to the house, maybe six feet above the roof.

Back then we were so thrilled to have a television set. We were perfectly happy and thrilled having only three channels, CBS, ABC, and NBC. All of them were in black & white showing on a picture tube of maybe two-feet by two-feet. We'd pretty much have that TV on most of the day and then come midnight the national anthem would play as the last thing you could watch until morning. I think it was around 1954 a whole new TV world opened up as color TV came about for our enjoyment! A whole new world for us kids for sure, can you imagine how it must have been for our parents? Not only for their own TV enjoyment and many of their special shows, the TV must have been a perfect pacifier for them!

I'd have to guess the *Howdy Doody* show was probably one of the first shows we watched at a young age, five, maybe six years old. That shit didn't last long for me as westerns started to come on, such as *Davey Crockett, Long Ranger, Rin Tin Tin*, and *Maverick* to other hero shows like *Superman* and *Zorro* or much funnier shows than Doody, like *Little Rascals, I love Lucy*, and *Laurel & Hardy*! Oh shit, I always love Laurel and Hardy movies, as they always had some great and witty slapstick comedy!

Loving "slapstick" comedy myself, I have to tell my favorite *Laurel and Hardy* scene from one of their episodes: The movie was when the two buddies were in prison and attending a mandatory physiology class. The instructor was the character actor that was in so many of Laurel and Hardy's movies, James Finlayson, the short bald guy with a very large mustache and always looked at Stan and Laurel with one eye squeezed shut, as if so irritated by the two knuckleheads. So the professor was discussing and testing the class about the universe, space, and the galaxies and he asked the question: Does anyone know what a comet is? Stan with that stupid grin raised his hand as if he knew the answer. The professor looked at him with his one eye shut, knowing better to let Stan answer this question picked another inmate to answer. The other convict stated, "A comet is a star with a tail behind it," and of course the professor said, "That's right." Now the professor asked the next question, "Can anyone name one," and of course Stan excitingly raises his hand as if for sure knowing the answer. So the professor, looking at him again, with his one eye squinting tightly, as if thinking this goofball can't screw this answer up, pointed at Stanly and says, "Okay, name one?" So Stan with his silly looking, confidant grin, so sure he's got this question, says, "Rin Tin Tin" (a star with a tail, love it). My all-time favorite Laurel and Hardy!

I would have to say the most popular and most watched TV show throughout the late fifties and sixties, at least for the young kids, not only around our China Lake Base but throughout the country, say from the age of twelve years old and up to the age of eighteen, was *American Bandstand* with its host, the "ageless" Dick Clark, on every Saturday early afternoon and was nationally televised from Philadelphia. I always remember Bandstand on Saturdays for an hour 12:30 to 1:30 P.M., although, I don't remember but have read *American Bandstand* was on five days a week! Always having the top current rock & roll songs, dances, and guest entertainers with their top hits of the time. I'm sure many fans still today can remember some of the more popular names of the shows unpolished teen regulars dancing and showing off the latest fashions in clothing and hairstyles!

I think back to what was my favorite sitcom's that I watched early in my TV life, there were two that I always remember growing up with. *The Adventures of Ozzie and Harriet* and *The Donna Reed Show.*

The real-life stories of Ozzie and Harriet Nelson and their all-American family. There was the retired musician Dad, Ozzie, and his wife, the motherly Harriet. Then the oldest son David, always the smart guy that you knew was going to turn out to be a Lawyer. Then the youngest of the Nelson family, the "irrepressible" Ricky who was around my age, maybe a few years older and just full of funny wise cracks. I felt he was the star of the show. Ricky, being similar in age made it so easy to relate, as I grew through the years with him. The best episodes to me, of course, was in Ricky's late teen years when he began playing the guitar and singing on the show. He was absolutely one of my favorite singers in the country and defiantly a "Teen Age Idol" of all the teenyboppers across America. I will always remember the time back in sixth grade, maybe thirteen years old or so, and Jimmy Thomas, Gary Massaro, and I were invited over to Karen Markers house over on Independence Street for a Saturday night backyard party. Gary and Jimmy, both with thick, very dark hair, dressed as Elvis and I tried to look something like Ricky. Massaro was a really good-looking guy anyway and without trying had a young Elvis look. Jimmy was much bigger but had natural thick dark hair and a chubby, cute Elvis look. As for me, well, I didn't know shit about music, singing, or playing a guitar, but I did know how to have fun, joke and be a wise guy like Ricky. I could easily pretend that I could sing. Hell, that's all Karen and her gang of girls wanted was for us to, what we called back then, pantomime or lip sync, as it's referred to today the latest hits from the idols of that time. Elvis and Ricky Nelson being two! So the three of us with guitars in hand, our collars up, and shirts with a couple buttons unbuttoned did our best to be teenage idols and thrill the girls for the night. It certainly worked because we all had a ball doing our thing as the girls did some lady idol songs and thrilled us guys! That was a lot of fun being Ricky for an evening…

The Donna Reed Show, another family style sitcom about a young wife, the famous Donna Reed as Mrs. Donna Stone the housewife of husband Dr. Alex Stone as they face ventures with their two kids Mary and Jeff. I actually started watching this show a little later about the time I was more interested in girls, maybe eight, Ha Ha, no, just kidding. Maybe fourteen or so and as the pretty Mary, actress Shelley Fabares (also played Christine, the beautiful wife of Coach Haden Fox on the sitcom *Coach*) was late in her teens, began singing on the show. Man, when she first sang "Johnny Angel" that was it, I mean I was totally in love. I knew she was singing that song just for me…right. Actually, except for Donna Reed, who I always liked as an actress, Mary singing was the only real interest I had watching the show.

I do remember some of my parent's favorite TV programs, only because if I didn't like them, well, tough shit. Ha-Ha. Seriously, we usually liked anything that you could watch on TV back in the early days of television, even if it was some squirrely program like *The Lawrence Welk Show* that we had to watch throughout the fifties and into the sixties. I do remember the only part of that show I always liked was when the beautiful Lennon Sisters came on to sing. I'll always remember those pretty ladies' eyes would twinkle as if there were stars in them. I'm sure most folks from the Indian Well Valley knew that our Burros football coach in the sixties, Coach Bruce Bernhardi's brother Lee was married to a Lennon sister, I believe Janet Lennon.

A few other programs in the fifties my parents watched, one of course came on every Sunday night, *The Ed Sullivan Show*. I have to say all us kids liked watching the Sullivan show, especially when we knew he was bringing on rock-roll idols. Of course, two most famous that I'll always remember watching, as I'm sure every kid from eight to twenty tuned-in for. On September 9, 1956 when Elvis Presly rocked on to the Sullivan scene, although viewed from the waist up, Elvis shock the young world up like no other.

I'd have to believe if any group could outdo the great Elvis, it had to be when the British phenoms from Liverpool, the Beatles erupted on the US shores by way of the Sullivan show on February 9, 1964. *The Red Skelton Show* was another fifties show my parents as well as us kids enjoyed watching together. Comedy was a huge entertainment in our family.

Into the sixties my parents had even more varity shows to enjoy, program's such as *The Andy Williams Show*, *The Carol Burnett Show*, and *The Dean Martin Show*. Dean Martin was always my Dad's favorite, as it was mine!

CHAPTER 8
Annual/Special Events

THE FIESTA

Back in the very early years, I remember the base held an annual, what I recall as "The Fiesta," and it was held out front in the huge west side parking lot of the Bennington Plaza in front of where the malt shop, Special Service Office, and the old post office were located. We were pretty little, so everything seemed larger than life. Gaming, ice cream, and other entertaining booths and a few little rides for the smaller kids like us. As far as I remember the carnival like Fiesta didn't last long, maybe a couple years but while it was there, it was pretty neat to us little guys.

THE FAIR

Like I said, the Fiesta didn't last long and really was hard to remember since it was when I was just a runt. I do remember the fair that would come to Ridgecrest every year in the springtime. Most likely why the small fiesta went away off the base. Our parents would take us for years to the fair, which was set-up on a large, empty piece of land on China Lake Blvd., just a block south of the K&R Market and Corey's shoe store and next to the ole A&W Root Beer stand, where the Home Depot sits today. I remember as a little guy how I thought it was so big with so many game booths and the biggest rides we'd ever seen!

My mind also barely recalls at least one time, and again when we were very little, so it's hard to be specific, but off base in Ridgecrest and west on Inyokern road about three quarters way to Inyokern, say six miles west from the Base front gate and along the railroad tracts that paralleled Inyokern road on the north base side. Just that one time I remember the famous Barnum & Baily circus was brought in on rail train, and I will assume by either the Navy Special Services or USO and had set up at least three huge, big tents including the main event inside the Big Top. I'm talking about all the jungle animals that you would typically expect at a circus. Animals such as many large elephants, lions, tigers, and giraffes along with clowns, games, and refreshment booths to go along with a spectator big top circus show, all controlled by the ring master with his large top hat and included riders performing tricks on the backs of horses, lion tamers with their long whips snapping at the lions, just like you'd always see in pictures or on TV. Really fascinating and obviously very memorable to us little desert kids growing up in the high desert.

ARMED FORCES DAY AND AIR SHOW

Every year China Lakers could depend on being entertained by the Navy's display of its mighty arsenal of aircraft weaponry, missiles, and rockets that actually would draw folks from all over Southern California for this very exciting event, Armed Forces Day. The line of cars and Navy tour buses winding out to the Armitage Field, later more referred to as just NAF (Naval Air Facility) would be miles long and you could anticipate at least an hour or more to get out to the airfield. I'm sure a huge weekend event for all the merchants in the Bases neighboring town of Ridgecrest. This event goes back as far as I can remember and I'm sure in some similar fashion continues today. In the old days when we were very young, Dad would always take the family out in the old station wagon and of course, as we got older in our teens, we'd always go out with our friends, usually the Rowe Street Gang. We'd take a Navy tour bus or one of our parents would take us out, and we'd just go off on our own to frolic in the huge crowd. Back then the Navy would really do it up well, as their jet aircraft demonstrations would include many air-to-surface firings at old truck or tank targets or surface-to-air shots and their exploding drone targets a few thousand yards out in front of the estimated 100,000 or so excited crowd. Just a great several hours of aircraft demonstrations, games, and refreshment booths. The weather was usually hotter than shit for this spectacular Navy show. The highlight, always ending with the Navy's Blue Angels, one by one slowly rolling off their exhibition parking spot toward the runway and one by one taking off in front of the roaring crowd, to join up together to give the huge crowd a true patriotic final demonstration of naval aviation at its finest is still hard to forget. Go Navy!

Early crowd at the Armed Forces Day show

COMPTON CUTIES

Several times, maybe a two-year span, sometime in the mid to late fifties, the Base, through Special Services, brought in a novelty softball team composed of men dressed in ladies' garments. I remember watching this team twice, two years in a roll play one of the Base's softball teams, or an all-star team from the Base's softball league! This team called the Compton Cuties out of Southern California was made up of what were very obviously excellent baseball players as well funnier than shit comedians! The most memorable of these players was always this little Mexican midget on the team. Though-out the evening he, oops, I mean she, would be sneaking around, not just on the field but in the stands amongst audience. Constantly pinching the Navy players in the ass and running off. This little shit, all dressed up in ladies' garb, just going around harassing everyone!

All dressed in women's funny 'show-time stage clothing, hats, glasses, and fake lady wigs brought laugh-provoking comedy to the Schoeffel Field crowd against our own good-natured Navy softball players. If you were lucky enough to have experienced these funny but most talented athletes/comedians, it was a show you would still remember. I'll always re-member in their warm-ups, which was the major part of the show before the game, where during the warm-up anything spontaneous could happen and usually did all in the fun of the game. The warm-ups included many individual and group act's showing off their abilities and tricks. My all-time favorite I'll never forget is after the coach took outfield warm-ups, includ-ing a funny little show, where theses outfielders showed off their abilities along with some funny shit; they would start the infield warm-ups with all the infielders in their positions.

They would do "round-the-horn" as if they were throwing the ball around, but they did it so quick, I mean like lighting fast, you couldn't see the ball! Right! Well, they didn't have a ball, which of course we didn't know at the time. Just before each fielder caught the imaginary ball from the other position player, he'd hit his glove with his throwing hand as if the ball just came in his mitt and at the same time he was throwing it to the next position player as it continued round-the-horn they all did it is the same similar manner. This was done so well it looked like the real thing but faster than the eye could see! So here's these funny dressed ladies having infield, includ-ing this lighting speed "round the horn," and at the same time, all of them just jawing and joking like "Ho-Hmm" a gaggle of women! Just funnier than shit. I'm sure something similar would go over just as well today as back them. Just a great gimmick!

Any of you remember seeing the Compton Cuties?

California Cuties - softball Team 1955

WEATHER RELATED

Another huge event not only on base but throughout the high desert would happen I'd say every three to five years and that was the incredible snow storms the winter would bring to the valley on occasion. No way close to the amounts the High Sierra mountain range would receive every year, but down on the valley floor, we'd get some pretty darn nice snow, unlike the mountain or the east coast folks, who receive so much every year that they would just get down-right sick of it. So much snow! Well, not the China Lake folks, everyone from the kids to the parents all love to see the snow come in. As kids we pretty much or at least had a good feeling when it was close to snowing, not to say we also had some surprised storms, but we'd get all excited in anticipation for it to happen. I'm not so sure, though, if the excitement was because of the actual snow or that the Base school district would always shutdown and close the schools for the first several days of the storm.

For me it was the snow but certainly happy for the fun-in-the-snow time off from school. There were also occasions that the Navy would shout the whole Base down due to very heavy snow. I remember such a storm back in the late fifties that snowed so hard and for several days no one could even drive. I mean like five feet or so of snow that stayed on the ground several weeks, always a wonderful surprise and fun time when winter brought in the snow to the Base!

Independence Street in the early days

Another annual weather-related occurrence in our desert which usually occurred several times in the hot, dry summer months that I myself loved and have often heard many desert folks say the same is the special smell you would get after a good summer rain. The smell of the soaked Mojave Desert wet Creosote bush and its refreshing virgin oil sent, as if these normally very dry greasewoods throughout the summer heat, would actually come to life, opening up its joy with this welcomed desert moisture from above, together expressing happiness with its distinct smell throughout the desert for a few hours. Such a refreshing smell you can find only in the Mojave Desert!

I'm going to say it now, yes, as I reminisce growing up on Base, there were only two things that irritated me, hated more than anything and both relate to weather. The wind, of course, was a total menace to everyone who ever lived in the high desert of California. The desert windstorms were the most irritating of all weather related, let's just say headaches or better yet, migraines! There is no one in the history of the Base that could say they liked the winds. We just had to put up with them, no ifs, ands, or buts about it.

The other irritable menace living in the desert unless you never played outside barefooted was those four or five prong Stickers or Goat Heads. They just seemed to be everywhere, waiting in batches for the next human kid to step on with their bare feet! These little pricks had to have some kind of poison on the tips of each of its devilish prong's that would make entrance into the skin twice the hurt. Try pulling then out with the fingers only meant more frickin' pain as they enter the skin of the fingers! Just one was a horrible experience, but no, they had to cluster and make it a family affair! One could figure at least ten minutes delay while pulling these horned little devils out of the foot and then hand! Even those big red ants weren't as bad as the stickers. The red ant had a rough bite, causing a nice welt but they always worked along, not in clusters. There was even a positive with the red ant's, making an ant farm creating quite an interesting science project. Nope, not the goat head, they just wanted cause evil. Seriously!

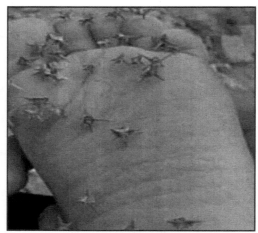

The Devil's Menace

POTATO CHIP

Many summer's heavy rainstorms brought desert flash floods to the Base but more predominately in rural areas of the upper desert, where the most danger occurred as the flood waters would cross and damage highways. I recall many times heading either north or south from the Base on Highway 14, mainly during the summer months when we'd be delayed by highway patrol and had to drive very cautiously through the strong flowing rain flooded roadways. Back on the Base, well, the Rowe Street Gang kind of looked forward to the down pours in anticipation of flash floods, just not only to run and jump in, at least the smaller ones, but also, we had found a place pretty far out in the desert out close to the back gate that we named "Potato Chip," a very large, natural catch basin. For years when the heavy summer rains would show up, it would always create a little flash flood run of water from somewhere out of the west desert, before, but where the Burroughs High School was built in the late fifties. We would always head out to Potato Chip, knowing that it would be filled with water maybe five feet deep or so. Perfect for the raft we made out of an old broken up telephone pole we found around the area and some two by six's we brought out with us. Always a fun, Tom Saylor type venture. AND then they built the high school and cut off the flow of flash flood water, ending our many summer's desert lake venture. Oh yeah! So you ask why the name Potato Chip? Sorry! Well, very simply, once the catch basin finally dried up many days after a rainstorm, it would always leave broken up clay-like desert mud that, when hardened, broke or cracked up into little pieces that looked like thousands of large potato chips, so, that's what we named this fun little swimming hole! Hello.

DESERT WHIRLWIND'S OR DUST DEVILS

There was another little fun toy created by the weather that we, the Rowe Street Gang, always looked forward to competing against each other for who had the balls to fight these little dirty, stinging tornados looking beast. Yep! I'm talking chasing down and jumping into the desert whirlwind, better known as a dust devil. Most people know and have seen dust devils that strong, well-formed and relatively short-lived and harmless desert whirlwind. I should use "harmless" in this case very lightly, as I can tell, yeah, some of the dust devil's we have jumped in did some pretty good harm! I remember up in the dirt playground yards of Vieweg School one Saturday afternoon, Roger jumped in a pretty big dust devil and this prick pulled him into the air, high off his feet while spinning him around like a top, completely out of control in this mini-tornado. Well, the only thing that came between him flying off to "who knows where" was the playground's six-foot chain-link fence. I mean he flew into that fence going like thirty miles an hour and damn near knocked himself out, certainly left some pretty nice cuts and bruises! It actually looked kind of fun, but I just couldn't catch up with the little monster to jump in with Roger. That bet cost me seventy-five cents, well worth it as I think about it today. Right?

HALLOWEEN

October 31st of every year was a huge day for all the kids of the Base, including the Rowe Street Gang. Every neighborhood on Base in all the different housing communities, just around five o'clock in the evening and through the night until maybe around 10 P.M., the streets were packed with kids of all ages and all dressed in their scariest costumes and carrying the bag of collected candy and the sort as they trick-or-treated to every door. The youngest kids, of course, escorted by their parents. These unbelievable crowds of kids on every block, at least at every block the gang went too and that was a lot! I would more than assume that this large crowds of kids had to be the same at every neighborhood on Base. I have often thought all those lit streetlight neighborhood blocks, full of kids in costumes, trick-or-treating door to door, would be a perfect Norman Rockwell painting! I also have wondered if this type of participation for trick-or-treating was similar in cities and towns around the country back in the fifties. I mean there were just so many kids out trick-or-treating this special night each year. I'd be even more curious of maybe, if in fact, there was just so much more patriotism on this military base during these years creating all this enthusiasm for these events, including, standing for the national anthem before all movies at the Base theater! I'm talking of unbelievable participation from **all** the Base residents. AGAIN, JUST CURIOUS!

The Rowe Street Gang pretty much went trick-or-treating together every year during the time we all lived in the Rowe Street neighborhood. We each usually brought an extra grocery bag or pillowcase and several different costumes, or at least parts of another, like a wig or hat, something to change our costume a bit for the second round at the same door! Every year one of us would have some firecrackers to let off and excite all the kids as they trick-or-treated. One time I think it was Bobby who brought along a cherry bomb, if you know what these are and how fucking powerful the little pricks were. Anyway, we were up in another territory and some guy had his mailbox in front of his yard by the road, so Bobby put the cherry bomb in this mailbox, and after making sure no one was close around to the blast area, he lit it as we all scrambled in different directions. In about five seconds this damn thing went off with a huge bang and blew that mailbox clean off its stand and into the night air along with a large puff of smoke, scaring the crap out of everyone in and around the block, including people in their houses. I ran up to a house two doors down and up on the porch as if I was just trick-or-treating, at the same time the man who came out his front door must have seen me with the guys around the mailbox and knew I was with the little shits that lit the bomb. He grabbed my arm and tried to pull me into his house while hollering to his wife to call police! Oh shit, he wasn't going to get me in his fucking house, so I kicked the guy in the crouch while pulling away and finally once loose, jumped off his porch and ran into the night. I mean I was only maybe ten years old or so, what the hell, the damn bully! Ha Ha. Well, we all finally met up with each other a while later and had a good laugh of how loud that cherry bomb was and the damage and smoke it created and of course me almost getting caught as we trick-or-treated are way back home. We didn't mess with cherry bombs any more after that episode! As usual "A good night of tricks and a whole bunch of treats"! Hey! That was just one year! Ha Ha.

ATOMIC EXPLOSIONS FROM NEVADA

Now, here's a pretty cool story that happen to me a few years back in 2005 or so that made my mind take off in fine reminiscing form to my young days at China Lake that most kids on Base can relate too! I stood looking over this massive crater, maybe a half mile across and some thousand feet deep located at the Nevada Test Site at Mercury, currently Nevada National Security Site some 65 miles north of Las Vegas, Nevada. On a site visit with other industry contractors of this special, former atomic test site over seen by US Department of Energy we were given a surprise tour of this massive crater. Most likely special to the other bus load of contractor representatives but to me, so much more!

As I stood on top of this massive crater my mind just took off, heading straight back into the late 1950's and even more specific July of 1962, when this huge hole in the ground was created. I so well remember my dad back in that time, starting earlier in the late fifties and having us kids all out in the front yard grass, getting us all pumped up in anticipation for the bright light flashes from the national advertised atomic explosion that was to occur that evening at a specific time just over the B Mountain. The first couple bright flash occurrences we witnessed was in the late fifties, what we understood were more of a smaller version from the huge explosion we witnessed just over B Mountain that mid evening of July of 1962, and what created this crater. My Dad from all he heard seemed to be a little worried maybe even nerves about us kids looking directly at the flash at detonation from over the skies of Nevada as this was advertised as the biggest of all atomic explosions, so my dad had acquired some dark film for us to watch the blast's flash through. Pretty darn exciding to us kids around the Base as we did understand that the Navy at China Lake along with their counterparts at White Sands Missile Range in New Mexico had a huge part in the design and testing of the atom bomb!

THE TEHACHAPI EARTHQUAKE

This major earthquake happened in 1952 and was registered as a 7.3 on the richter scale, centered around the town of Tehachapi, some fifty miles east of Bakersfield, California and approximately one hundred miles west of China Lake. So 1952 makes me four years old, how in the hell do I still remember it rocking & shaking our home on Base? I remember Mom yelling earthquake and to get into a doorway! I can still picture myself as I stood in underwear with my hands on each side of my bedroom doorway, as I shock back and forth for maybe a minute or so for what felt like an eternity! It must have had a huge effect on me subconsciously if I can remember and still picture small parts of that earthquake so long ago!

This earthquake was the largest in the continental United States since the San Francisco Earthquake of 1906. It claimed twelve lives and caused property damage estimated at $60 million dollars.

THE PRESIDENT'S VISIT

I have to say one of the biggest events that had ever come to the Base was when our 35th President of the United States, John F Kennedy, came to China Lake in the summer of 1963, just five months prior to that dreadful day in Dallas, Texas in November of that year. I'm hoping to put this visit by one of America's most popular president's in modern history in perspective from the young local China Lakers and our excitement for those who didn't experience this historical visit to China Lake. The rumors started flowing not only around the Base but throughout Kern County several months before it was announced and verified. In my mind, politics, at least to the teenagers in the sixties before we were at the age to vote, was more about popularity than riding party lines, but for sure, all political candidates were highly respected. To us kids it was just go on about our day with the excitement of the possibility that the president may be coming sometime in the summer.

I remember my Dad was telling us back then and all the stories after the President's visit, what the Base went through in anticipation for the president actually coming to the Base and then at the time when the rumors became official. He was coming! Charlie often told his version of the story while reminiscing with others many times afterwards! His office had "fly over photos" of three different routes the Navy had projected or anticipated for the tour of the Base for the president. My dad said with approximately two months of time his contract's office was tasked to have all the buildings located on all three routes painted in time for the visit. They quickly contacted many of the painting contractors that were under painting contracts at that time on base or have worked previously on the base under painting contracts with the contract's office.

Once they located and determined contractors and with some sort of specifications, basically type of paint, colors, and location of building's to be painted, they direct awarded contracts to several painting contractors. As Charlie tells it with much laughter, the contractors were directed to paint only the street facing, the front sides of each building, and the two building sides and leave, **do not paint** the back of any of the buildings. Halfway through the number one priority route, it was determined that the second route was to be the official route. So they had to scramble over to the alternative route and precede in the same manner of painting as the first. Now this is just a small example of what the Navy must had been going through as told by my dad and just one situation that occurred in the contract's division. I just can't imagine back then as a teenager what a panic attack mode the Base was in, in preparation of their special guest. I did hear rumors that Public Works added on a new room to the captain of the Base's house, I believe Cpt. Blenman at #1 Enterprise, and named the room the "Kennedy Room." I also heard a rumor that the President didn't even stay overnight on Base but ended up in San Diego later that evening. Government spending at its best!

(Air Force One with President Kennedy at Armitage field)

Page Eight

Excitement Galore on Blandy

To this day the biggest topic of conversation, most likely for everyone, but for us teenagers pertaining to the Kennedy visit is "where were you setting or standing when President Kennedy came?" The President flew into the Naval Air Facility (NAF) in Air Force One to a very large cheering crowd. Everyone was informed by newspapers that his main route was going to bring him east on Blandy Avenue and up to the Officers Club for a luncheon with federal, state, Navy and local officials. You wouldn't believe the enthusiasm and great feeling of patriotism among ALL that was there this special day on Blandy Ave. "As if King Arthur's return to Camelot" as the crowd was some twenty deep on both sides of the road for the whole length, maybe 5 miles or so of Blandy to the O Club. I was with my brother Duke and Dikes (Sorge) and maybe one other and a few girlfriends, where we were sitting just in front of the Bank of America on the corner of Richmond Rd. and Blandy. A great and clear view of the President and his motorcade as they drove him buy in an open limousine. Just a great thrill, I must say! I can also say this with certainty as you read this story, and if you were there that special day, you're saying, "I know exactly where I was." OR you're thinking of that exact spot where you were! Right? Another story I heard secondhand was from Tommy Mather, as the motorcade was slowly driving up Blandy Ave., local high schooler, Gary Miller, ran out on to Blandy just as the president was passing, as he came close to the Presidents limo several secret service guys grabbed him, but the President waved them off and shock Millers hand! Definitely something from the past you would never see happen today.

My brother Roger is always excited to tell his story of that afternoon and just after the president had finished the special luncheon at the O Club and the Navy officials were giving the president a little tour of the SOQ housing as they drove around in a much smaller convoy of vehicles and the president in his open limousine as Roger and Doc Colloday's daughter, Carolyn were sitting up in her front yard lawn of her house which backs up to the Officers club pool, and is one of three houses and yards in, like a little circle off the main road for the SOQ's. So as just the two of them alone, Roger and Carolyn, were just sitting there visiting when the presidents tour came slowly driving by just in front of Roger and Carolyn and as the president slowly passed by he waved to the two of them as they set in the grass, and theywaved back to the president. Pretty cool story! Oh!

CHAPTER 9
The First Of The First

As I continue thinking about all the wonderful places and events, I've pretty much been talking of kids of my age group, including somewhat, those within five or six years of my age. There is actually another age group of first kids I've come to name here as the "First of the First" as I'm sure most came here as a young kid or teenager on Base before or during the Navy's housing explosion in the mid to late forties, experiencing much more of the infrastructure construction of this new military base compared to my age group when most of the construction had been completed, at least the earlier houses and support facility's. All ready for us, the newest and youngest desert rats coming up a few years later.

Many of these first kids graduated from the local high school and stayed around to work for the Navy on base, retired and still live in the valley. I have over the years gotten to know many of them fairly well. I've come to learn that they have many of the similar stories of growing up on base. As I did some research, and I use the word "some" loosely, from what I understand, it had been much more difficult than us kids coming up a little later in the early fifties. I mean hell, we had telephones, even though they were shared party lines. Those first kids had to share with their neighbors the same phone from an outside telephone pole. Some of those early birds had to share common showers and restrooms, some in Quonset Huts until their new house or apartments were ready to occupy. The newly planted trees they had were not big enough to shade a lizard, everything was still just desert dirt, hard pan, and hotter than hell. When my age group came in several years later those trees were fully grown and blossoming shade like you wouldn't believe, like a huge oasis.

Anyway, the point I want to bring out here is, yes, they did have it a little rougher, not to say they were complaining, no way, but many who I personally know, or know but didn't know they were a first China Laker, stayed in the Indian Well Valley area after graduating from the local high school at Burroughs. If they didn't go to college or came back home after college, they either went to work for the Navy on Base, or in the surrounding town, now the city of Ridgecrest. This special age group, the "First of the First," who most would be in their late seventies, maybe early eighties. These folks also, still today, speak so highly of their youth, tell so many stories and still reminisce with their lifelong friends, just the same as my age group does about growing up on Base at China Lake.

What I have found very interesting as I have read through Navy history and especially the China Lake/Ridgecrest local IWV "High Desert Memories" web-site, in its many posts of those "early to mid-1940's **First of the First** China Lake kids," is that most every written post, talk of the same "common" ventures, events, and places from their own personal experiences but in similar fashion, as I have been discussing here about my age group. I'm not just talking about a few, no I'm talking hundreds these elder China Lakers still living in the valley.

These written posts by those First China Lakers that I have recently stumbled across, basically, reinforces what I have been describing here from my age group perspective, us younger, let's say second of the first, those China Lake kids from my time in the late fourties through the fifties and mid-sixties. I thought it would be fun to add just a few of these "First of the First" kid's short stories, through their own words, experiences growing up in the earliest days at China Lake. Again, as we will see, many of the same ventures, places, and events I hope I have accurately and more important, "interestingly" described from my age group days! So let's just see what I come up with here. Hopefully, you will find as interesting....

This first story comes from excerpts of a much longer story by Roy Gerard, Burros Class of 1951:

"Some of my grade schooling was spent in the Quonset hut school at China Lake. I remember one of my teachers was small of stature but deadly with erasers. She could hit me in the back of the head from across the room.

Our family moved into a duplex at the corner of Nimitz Avenue and Richmond Road, just north of the first Bank of America. It was a wonderful home with steam heat. We lived there for many years, across the street from the St. George family. Frank was a schoolmate and is still a dear friend.

I graduated from the original "Burroughs" H/S in 1951. I spent almost all of my working career at China Lake, retiring in 1972. I met my wife, Roxie, at burros. She gave birth to my first two children at Drummond Hospital, in Ridgecrest. Rhonda lives in Southern California and Rita Jean is buried in the old Wolford Heights (Kernville) cemetery.

The old western town of Kernville, where I spent some of my youth, was a great place to beat the heat while the base was being built. It was inundated by Isabella Lake and I miss it. If anyone has old pictures of the town (before Isabella), I would sure like copies.

The people I met as acquaintances, co-workers, and friends throughout the desert area will never be forgotten. My memories of each of you are grand, indeed. I realize that the early years probably don't appeal to those who came later, but for me, they were the best ever.

To those who helped to build and work a NOTS, the "SECRET CITY"; bless you, each and everyone.

Did you know that there was an atomic blast set off at China Lake, even before those at Vegas (Yucca Flats)? Yep. It was much smaller than those that came later.

I now reside in the great State of Montana, some call it "the last best place." It is beautiful and cool, the early days and people of NOTS, however, were even better. The stories above are merely a portion of those I can offer to interested parties. I have so many others. Thank you for your time and interest."

Roy J Gerard

This story is from Phyllis Haig (Burros Class of 57) … although somewhat confusing by some of the dates and people mentioned, the comparison is still the intent…Also, I defiantly remember her parents. Actually, her Dad I had as my art teacher!

"So many wonderful memories coming back now. Ceci Schilberg and Ann Drummond have just contacted me for the 40-year reunion of Burroughs Class of 67, coming up in Nov. at Lake Tahoe.

My parents were teachers on base, mom was a PE teacher and dad was an eccentric art teacher with a wonderful open studio classroom. My sisters, Arlie, Laurie, and Tammy went to China Lake schools and Ian was born in Drummond. He was autistic and stayed with the Dixons when we lived on Tyler St.

Tammy and I used to take off from there for desert hikes to B Mountain on Saturdays, packing PB&J sandwiches and MILK. Hiking out past the dry lake and catching and releasing scorpions, "Horney" toads, tortoises, and blue bellies. Hardly waiting to get to the shade of those rocks in B Mtn. Then when it rained in the spring, the dry lake would have a couple inches of slippery silt we would "ice skate" in. That dry lake was where I later also learned to drive.

I remember the A-bomb scares, hiding under our desks to drill for when the Russians might drop the big one on us. Thank god for those desks, they would have given us great protection, huh?

Then there were the Princeton's and Steve Zissos and all his girlfriends and the dances so innocent (for some of us...) and the beginnings of the desert parties, such wide-open spaces.

Thanks to Dr. Tiffany I know how to write, thanks to his teaching us to diagram a sentence. And so many other great teachers.

The pool was my lifesaver, getting board-diving instructions that I later continued at the LA athletic club. We used to routinely walk up there from Sellers' Circle, sometimes BAREFOOT, stealing from shade spot to shade spot. I never could beat Anne Auld in swimming, I always got second. And Mrs. Chatterton, our swim coach, what a blessed woman. Anyone know where Jeannie and Terri Chatterton are?

I haven't been back since we moved in late 64, but am planning a trip soon. Would love to be able to get on base to see its changes but would need to be visiting someone, I understand. Oh well.

See you all at the reunion and beyond, hope to hear from anyone who recognizes the Haig name."

Phyllis Haig (Class of 57)

This last story from Mike Miller is short and sweet but pretty much some's it up...

What I really remember about growing up on the high desert was the availability to being able to just roam. We hiked to B mountain, walked all through Mirror Lake area, hunted lizards, snakes, and rabbits, and went up to the mountains to fish and play in the snow.

I remember one year at Easter time when it rained and rained and rained. So much that there were people actually in row boats in the streets! While the summers could get to 120 degrees the winters could me pretty cold. That darn wind blowing off the mountains chilled me many a morning and afternoon while walking to school.

What really impressed me at the time was the cost of everything on the Base. Movies, although infrequent, were only a dime! Saturday matinees were something all the kids had to attend. Beer parties, once we were in high school, were conducted out in the desert where no one could get hurt. Yes, growing up on the high desert was a fun affair. I can't even imagine how much trouble I would have gotten into doing the same things elsewhere that I was able to do on the desert. I wouldn't trade the experience for anything. Mike Miller

Ditto Mike...

SHORT STORIES FROM THE BASE

I liked these little, short stories so much about my home from the early days, not knowing these earlier "First of the First" China Lakers, but still, I can so relate to their stories. I thought I'd like to have some more fun with this but from around my time at China Lake. So, I went out on the internet to Facebook, where I still communicate with so many friends I grew up with, along with many I have become friends with much later in my life. I received some nice responses and have agreed to post a few of them here in this book for all to enjoy. Again, notice the similarities!

The first and I do believe my favorite is from Cindy Riggs. Now anyone who knows Cindy knows she doesn't like to do things small, likes to post photos of friends and family, especially from her past and even more specially from her life at China Lake and Burroughs High School days. She certainly doesn't let us down here with her story and photos.

GROWING UP ON THE NAVAL ORDNANCE TEST STATION (NOTS) CHINA LAKE FROM THE EYES OF CYNTHIA RIGGS DEEM

My father began working at China Lake in March of 1949. At that time, there was a lack of family housing so my family lived with my maternal grandparents in Riverside, California. My father would stay in a BOQ during the week and with us on weekends. I was born in October of 1949 and when family housing opened up on base, my family moved into 80-B Forrestal in March of 1950. I have no memory of that house. Pictured is my mother, Ditty Riggs in the doorway, my paternal grandfather, Louis Riggs, holding me with my sister, Fran, peeking over the fence, and my sister feeding me grapes. You can tell from the photos that the base housing was built quickly and without a lot of vegetation. We were, after all, out in the middle of the desert.

Around 1951, my family moved to 201-A Byrnes Street and lived there for about five years. I had neighbor playmates and attended Kindergarten at Murray School and first and second grade at Groves School. I remember walking to school with my sister and neighbors, learning to ride my two-wheeled bicycle, and playing in the sprinklers on our front lawn during the summer. We all knew our neighbors well and as kids would go from house to house, playing in both the front and back yards, which more times than not had more sand than grass, often going in whoever's house we were at to get snacks. Because of the safe environment in which we lived, all the kids would get together at Halloween to go trick-or-treating without parental supervision. We loved that freedom and only had to check in with our parents from time to time as the evening progressed. Here I am with my parents, sister, paternal grandparents, and maternal grandmother when we first moved into the house, my first day of Kindergarten, and me in a Halloween costume made by my mother. Because of where we lived, shopping was very limited, so my mother sewed most of my sister's and my clothes.

(First day of kindergarten.)

In November of 1956, we moved to 209-B Wasp Rd. I was in second grade so our move had me changing schools. Here, we lived across the street from Richmond Elementary and our house backed up to open desert, both of which led to many play adventures with my friends. Hours were spent exploring the desert and bringing home red racer snakes, lizards, "horny toads," and an occasional desert tortoise. All of which my mother made me "take back out to their home." I have two vivid memories of finding a snake in our hallway and having mom chase a lizard in the kitchen. She grew up a city girl so this new desert life was interesting, to say the least. For me, not knowing anything different, growing up on base in the desert was fun and normal. To this day, I hate wearing shoes since whenever the weather allowed, I went barefoot, as did most of the kids. We learned to avoid "goat head" stickers and always walked with our head down to watch where we put our feet. In the heat of the summer, I got really good at running across the asphalt street, stopping briefly on the white line in the middle. As the joke went, that you could fry an egg on the sidewalk, we actually tried it and it worked. The only problem we had was that we didn't have sidewalks so it was fried on the street. In the winter, when a very occasional snowstorm hit, school was closed and we spend the day playing with friends. That didn't happen very often, so when it did, the whole base came to a standstill.

(I'm in the white jacket and pink pants, watching someone get hit with snowballs.)

It was in this house where I became best friends with Beverly Shull. She lived just a couple houses down from me and if I wasn't at her house, she was at mine. Our big thing was to trade sandals. We must have thought the other person's shoes were better. Life-long friendships like ours was something of the norm for most of our friends. That's one thing that was unique about growing up at China Lake. My dad was a physicist and worked for Civil Service but was also in the Navy Reserves, ending his career as a commander. Many who worked at China Lake were active military, thus some of my friends lived at China Lake for only a few years. Even with those friends, bonds were made and I continue to stay in touch with several of them to this day.

(Beverly Shull and Cindy Riggs)

The Lippincott family was one of the active military families with whom my parents and I became close friends. Mom and I flew to New Hampshire to attend Leanne's wedding in 2008.

Except for one school year, 1957-58 when my dad worked at the Pentagon and we lived in Falls Church, VA, we lived in this house until 1962, at which time we moved to 713 Ticonderoga Avenue.

Because of the importance of technical discoveries and developments made at China Lake, our parents were highly educated and education of their children was a top priority. My parents in particular, kept up with all of my studies, much to my displeasure. I was an above average student but my interest laid in the social aspect of school, thus having fun walking to and from school with my friends was the highlight of my day. The BOQ (Bachelor Officer Quarters) was along our path, and if the morning was exceptionally cold, we would run the length of the hallway to stay out of the weather. We crossed our fingers that one of the men wouldn't step out of their room in their skivvies, or god forbid, completely naked. Then, on our way home, we'd stop off at the Navy Exchange or commissary and buy candy bars to eat on the remainder of our journey home. If we didn't get caught, we'd take turns pushing each other in a shopping cart and drop it off at the Commissioned Officers Mess Club at the top of the hill.

The summer months found my friends and me at the COM pool. When I turned 8 years old, and having passed a swim test, I was allowed to hop on my bike and go to the pool, accompanied by my older sister, until I was old enough to go alone. I was given a patch that my mother sewed onto my swim-suit, which showed that I could be there without parental supervision. My sister and I would spend the day swimming and hanging out with our friends. My mom would meet up with her friends at the pool and play bridge. Some-times, my Dad would join us after work. The adults would have happy hour at the Barefoot Bar while all the kids would still swim and have a great time. We would often stay for dinner at the snack bar and swim when it got dark. Those were the best of times! Here I am eating my favorite thing from the snack bar . . . French fries!

Murray Jr. High was the only jr. high on base. I'm not sure why this photo was taken, but someone round up a bunch of us for this photo. Pictured: Boy on left, Jimmy Jones. Front row L to R: Phyllis Haig, Cindy Riggs, Bret Har-ney, Susan Swanson, Karen Hughes. Second row: Beverly Shull, Robbie Kruse, Leanne Lippincott, Mark Metcalf. Back three girls: Ann Allen, Paula Williams, Margaret Allan.

Since China Lake was a Navy base, most everyone knew everyone, and thus there were many "watchful eyes," allowing us, as kids, to roam the base at will. I would often end up at the Saturday matinee with 2 dimes and a nickel in my pocket. A dime would go in the turnstile and I bought popcorn and a coke with the remainder. As soon as the lights went out, everyone would stand for the national anthem. Patriotic newsreels followed before they played the movie. Later on, when I had my driver license, if I happened to be driving by the admin building when they were either raising or lowering the flag, all traffic would pull over and stop while the national anthem was played. Sometimes we would even get out of the car and stand with our hand over our heart. When it was finished, we'd then go along our way. No one thought anything about it and it was the natural and right thing to do. Once I had the freedom of driving off base and around Ridgecrest, rules of where I could or could not go, were strictly enforced by my parents. For instance, I could go to the A & W Root Beer drive in with friends but was not allowed to go to the drive-in theater.

Our high school years brought all of the kids that were raised on the base and those who lived "out in town" (Ridgecrest) together. More friendships were made and over the years, our class reunions were well attended. Here I am at my 50th High School Class Reunion, with four of my kindergarten classmates.

For me, since I lived on base and the high school (Sherman E. Burroughs High School) was outside the base, I had to park in the dirt lot on the base side of the fence and walk through a guard gate. When returning to my car after school, I had to show my base pass to get back on the base.

The guard gate with B Mountain in the background. Each year, the senior class would white wash the B (which stands for Burroughs),

One thing that was not lacking was the abundance of sand. Since girls weren't allowed to wear pants to school, I still have vivid memories of the blowing sand, pitting the backs of my legs, and getting in my eyes, which was horrible since I wore contact lenses. Running the track during P.E. in an ugly one-piece white gym suit was the worst! But all the students had to do it so misery loved company!

As mentioned before, school for me was more social than educational. I have many fond memories of my times with friends attending dances, games, and school events. I was fortunate to be a songleader and my parents attended all of the games to support me and our school. School spirit was high among those in our community.

I am sitting in the grass area in front of the Administration building a BHS with the arched gym in the background.

The main quad area of BHS.

Mementoes from Pep Club and Song leading.

After graduation, I was off to college and on to the next chapter of my life but also retaining life-long friendships and memories of growing up at China Lake.

This next story is from a girl I grew up with through the years, graduated together in the Class of 66, Janice Little

MEMORIES OF CHINA LAKE

BY JANICE LITTLE

Looking back, my life at China Lake was "Stand by Me" as a child and "American Graffiti" as a teenager. I understood at age four, when we moved there in winter, 1952, it was in the "middle of nowhere" to quote my mom. (She lamented leaving Coronado!) It seemed like a place "without much." But it offered so much more.

With no extended family around, we developed close family friendships that endure to this day (65+ years)! We shared holidays with some for two decades. We still feel like family with our old friends.

With no crime, we could exercise enormous freedom even as young kids. We roamed the desert with friends, biked all over the base or town, stayed out late on summer's evenings, and went to the Club pool without our mother's watching. We walked to the movies with our base pass on a string around our neck and ten cents to get in plus ten cents for candy.

With just two grade school districts and one high school, we all learned together. Some of us started kindergarten, ended high school, and went to college together! We played sports, studied, danced, joked, and enjoyed time with our lifelong school buddies. (We did lament when our Navy friends moved.)

With no city or beach around, we learned to enjoy the beauty of the desert, the peaks of the High Sierra, and the lakes, streams, and canyons where we could vacation or just go hike and picnic on Sunday.

With no visibly rich people or big houses or big malls around for comparison, we lived modestly without feeling deprived. We had what we needed; sometimes we also got what we really wanted by going to the small local stores owned by people we knew!

With no information to go on, we still understood that what was invented and tested at China Lake was very important. We memorized and can still repeat the billboard security warning! In our pre-teens we learned some of the earlier secrets and knew why we were high on the Soviet's bombing target list. We were scared but also felt safe and secure. We knew our parents were contributing to America's superiority and safety.

We were without a number of things that others enjoyed, but we had so much more in our life in China Lake!

This story pretty much sums up living on Base at China Lake in the fifties and sixties. This short but precise story comes from Burroughs Class of 1965, Darlene Rhyn Holler.

(Untitled)

By Darlene Rhyn Holler

My family arrived on Base at China Lake in 1950, when I was 3 years old. Although we lived in several different houses the first few years, being so young I can't remember the earliest of them. Once my younger brother was born my parents qualified for a three-bedroom house and we moved into a three-bedroom duplex on Rebalo street, just a mile or so north of Vieweg school at the far west end of Base housing.

Living on Base was wonderful, so safe! We never had to lock our doors at night, including the car and even left the keys in the ignition as the car set in front of the house since we had no gauge. There were many different housing types on Base with names like Prefabs, Normac's, Pink-brick, Old Duplex's, Wherry's, and Capehart's. All the streets were named after Navy carriers and ships or famous Navy officers.

I remember everyone being very patriotic, like standing for the "Star-Spangled Banner" before the movies at the Base theater or stopping at the administration building every morning and evening as the national anthem would play, starting and ending the day.

We were so self-contained on the Base, are own commissary, Navy Exchange, theater, bowling alley, and so much more all located in one shopping plaza. Depending on your dad's Government Service rating (GS rating) determined the Club and pool type you could belong to. The higher the rating the nicer the club. (Officers, chief's or enlisted Men's Club.)

The unusual Bowling Alley at the Plaza next to the Gym and indoor pool had only three lanes and needed pinsetters. I remember my good friend, Mike Drake, was a pinsetter.

Just south of the Plaza, who could ever forget Murray Jr High school and how different junior high school was from all the elementary schools we all went to prior to Murray. Murray School brought all us same age kids around the Base together for the first time. I so remember our PE teacher, Mrs. McClain, would open up the girls PE hut during lunch time, referred to it as the "Campus Corner" for the kids to dance to the latest top hits blaring across campus!

I have so many memories, I could spend a week writing about them! I am so, so blessed to have so many friends, still today from those wonderful days at China Lake. It was like this special place, this Navy Base housing area at China Lake was built just for us kids growing up at that special time! I just loved how always feeling so safe and everyone knowing each other and being so friendly.

Thanks Mom and Dad...

Our last one is from an old friend of mine, Karen "Marker" Mather.

(UNTITLED)

BY KAREN "MARKER" MATHER

I was raised in China Lake/Ridgecrest, California, Kern County, during a time when most everyone treated each other with respect. We didn't eat a lot of fast food because it was considered a treat, not a food group. We drank Kool-Aid and ice tea made from water that came from our kitchen sink. We ate bologna sandwiches, peanut butter sandwiches, grilled cheese sandwiches, hot dogs, pot pies, but mostly homemade meals consisting of mainly meat, potatoes, beans, home grown vegetables, bread and butter, and homemade dessert. School lunches were delicious. Sometimes, for a special treat, we got to take our lunches to school in a brown paper bag or a lunch box.

We grew up during a time when we would gather glass bottles to take to the store and use the deposit money to buy penny candy. (We even got a brown paper bag to put the candy in). You could get a lot for just 25 cents. We also mowed lawns, helped neighbors with chores, and worked in the garden in the summer. We went outside to play games, ride bikes, run with siblings, cousins, and friends. We played hide and seek, kick the can, jump rope, hopscotch, Red Rover, red light, Mother, May I, kickball, basketball and dodge ball. We drank tap water from the hose outside... bottled water was unheard of.

We ate a hot breakfast or cold cereal at the breakfast table before going to school. We had no cable TV, just a couple channels, no microwave, or cell phones. We watched TV as a family: Gunsmoke, Gilligan's Island, Wonderful World of Disney, Bonanza, Mutual of Omaha's Wild Kingdom, Red Skelton, and Ed Sullivan. After school, we came home and did homework and chores and watched some cartoons on Saturday morning.

If we were bad in school, we got in trouble there. When we got home, we got in trouble again (because your parents already knew). Paddling was allowed in school and you behaved yourself or else.

We would ride our bikes for hours, and talk and play outside until the lightning bugs came out, or the street lights came on. We would catch bugs in mason jars, make mud pies, play in the water sprinklers, and pick wildflowers and four-leaf clovers.

We LEARNED FROM our parents and grandparents instead of disrespecting them and treating them as if they knew nothing. What they said was the gospel.

If someone had a fight, that's what it was - a fist fight and you were back to being friends afterwards and the bullying pretty much ceased. Kids that were around guns were taught how to properly use them and to respect them and never thought of taking a life.

We had to be close enough to home to hear Mom yelling or Dad whistling to tell you it's time to come home for dinner. We ate around the dinner table and talked to each other as a family unit. We said the Pledge of Allegiance, stood for the National Anthem and listened to our teachers.

We watched what we said around our elders because we knew If we DIS-RESPECTED any grown up we would get our behinds whipped. It wasn't called abuse. It was called discipline! We held doors for others, carried groceries, and gave up our seat to someone else without being asked.

We didn't hear curse words on the radio in songs or TV. If you cursed and got caught, you had a bar of soap stuck in your mouth and had to stand in the corner for quite some time. "Please, Thank you, Yes Ma'am and Yes, Sir" were part of our daily vocabulary!

We grew up with good, God-loving families. If we missed school or church, we had to stay inside all day. We couldn't leave the house or watch TV.

MY POEM

It's kind of funny that four years prior to me deciding to even write about my great adolescent and teenage life experience on Base at China Lake. I wrote a poem, mixed as a song to introduce this fun idea to our Class of 1966's 50-year re-union that occurred in Ridgecrest back in 2016. I named my poem "Desert Folk-Like you and Me" and formatted it after the great Don Williams song "Good Ole Boys Like Me."

We put together a kind of skit as part of that night's entertainment program. Classmate and good friend Jimmy Kline and his very well-known and famous "139th Street Barber Shop Quartet" voice beautifully sang each chorus between **me reading through the verses** with help from two beautiful classmates I re-crewed, Linda Taves and Dorothy Foster, singing to bridge a few of the verses just before Jimmy's chorus. The last verse we all four sang together to end the skit.

I thought it would be an enjoyable read to add our fifty-year re-union poem, "Desert Folks Like you and Me." Hmm, you may notice some similarities to everything else that has been written in this book!

"DESERT FOLK LIKE YOU AND ME" BHS CLASS OF 1966
BY J.C. MARTIN

The war had ended in Victory but not all came back. They fought and died for freedom after being attacked. Their "Rendezvous with Destiny" was won on foreign sand, once again liberty and freedom rang out across our great land. United by common value, no reason to look back, the greatest generation moved forward, getting their lives back on track.

Oh, how hot and dry was California's high desert valley Where our folks settled right in....so eager to rally. Guided by faith they jumped in with both feet, in support of our Navy as it built its new fleet. It was here they started families, they didn't hesitate HOME they called Ridgecrest, NOTS China Lake.

Like thoroughbred horses coming out of the gate, around the year of our lord...NINETEEN FORTY-EIGHT No matter what year you arrived in the mix, the journey was on for the Burros class of 66.

I can still see those star-filled skies on a hot summer night, those forgotten years still come back a lot to me. I guess we turned out to be what we're supposed to be and hopefully we made a difference in the lives we lead.

Looking back, each in our own different way, like I still remember little leagues opening day, 4th of July fireworks on the dry lake bed, or the great air shows, as the Navy showed off its lead. Being picked for all-stars was a boy's summer dream, As the girls competed for Miss Little League Queen. And, how can you forget back in those times That the old base theater movies only cost a dime! We'd leave home early and lizard hunt all day, back in by dark, never losing our way.

So many different schools as the years flew by and then off to Monroe or Murray Jr. High. From adolescence to teenage idols, PE dress and Home Economics, the Campus Corner, Bauer's' Burgers, Organized sports against each other...

Our last four years we grew up quick, and our class became our own little click. That "B" on the mountain taught us loyalty and pride for the Green and White colors of our local Burros High.

Friday night football, the aftergame dance, The same ol' thing for every home stance. Then, cruising the Blvd with your favorite friends, back and forth from Fosters and the Root Beer stand, as everyone awaited that nights PLAN.... Then head on out, into the black desert night, like following a string of runway lights. It's so hard to recall, all those desert outings But, we'll never forget the late-night sound of That "ol' Wolf Man howling"

The howl of the coyote we learned not to fear as we grew up in the desert year by year. Fate brought us together out here in the sticks as together we became. Burro's class of 1966.

I can still see the star-filled sky on hot summer's night and those forgotten years still come back a lot to me. I guess we turned out to be what we're supposed to be and hopefully we made a difference in the lives we lead. That's who we our...us desert folk, like you and me.

When we were in school life seemed so simple each day, although there were many tears shed along the way. That tragic morning in '63, never will we forget that November day. We lost a few buddies to that crazy Asian war, as they went off to do their patriotic chore. Our memories have faded over the past 50 years but their faces endure through the pain and tears. After graduation, lord we all hit the road and it really didn't matter how far away...we would go:

We can still see the star-filled sky on a hot desert night and those forgotten years still come back a lot to me. I guess we turned out to be what we're supposed to be and hopefully we made a difference in the lives we lead. That's who we are, us desert folk, like you and me. Yeah, that's who we are, just desert folk, like you and me....

Tribute To The Greatest Generation

As I brought to light in chapter one, when I began writing in March of 2020 while isolated in the middle of a world-wide pandemic, constituting a national emergency for the United States, much like the turmoil created after our country was deliberately attacked at Pearl Harbor almost eighty years ago, the world as we knew it has been turned upside-down. Yet, battling this microscopic enemy certainly is much different than World War II, but there are similarities. History has been written through time for that great generation's dealing with desperate situations. As for now, well, we are all called to reflect on who we are and who we will be for our family, community, country, and the world in a time crisis. There will only be history to judge how we respond as a country. I can only hope and pray that we Americans together look to that greatest generations values, personal responsibility and commitment, as our model to concur and triumph over the greatest threat of our time, this Chinese delivered Coronavirus-19.

I've always believed that hardships, mishaps, and tragedy in life will form true character, if this is true then those folks born between 1900 and 1924, who witnessed and endured the Great Depression and a world war, certainly earned their charter badges. It all changed during World War II, when a new era of American power and wealth arose with vengeance, creating one of the most prosperous eras in American history. The country settled into this new-found prosperity, marking some of the most pivotal times in our country's history, beginning with the start of the baby boomers era on through the fifties and into the sixties, bestowing theses values to their children, the youth of that time. Together with our reason but, most importantly, through what was required to be taught in the schools: American pride and honor in country, sacrifice and frugality, experiencing war-time rationing meant creativity in frugal living. I have no doubt their hard times in their lives created a work ethic that represented the greatest generation and passed on to the next generation, us baby boomers! This positive attitude and integrity, along with newfound power and wealth that came from a population with personal experience of hardship, created a country of happiness, honesty, and a wonderful atmosphere of idyllic peace at the turn of the decade into the fifties and sixties. An era in American history remembered with so much clarity as I write in this book and referred to as our time of Camelot.

I feel very strongly, more so over the past few years as we continue losing these great folks, for some ingenious way of thanking these unselfish, American patriots, men and women alike, who together sacrificed their lives from world tyranny so the future of their beloved country, their families, and all future Americans to live in peace! I wonder, just maybe, I can find that answer to these adamant feeling if others out there, not just who reads this story but every baby boomer still alive and future generations to come feel the same love as I do about this great generation.

When I say something ingenious, I mean so unique and special, something not just one person could handle but a nation as a whole would have to be some way involved, at least financially. Maybe by a tax, I don't know but defiantly government involvement would be needed. Here are those thoughts.

So over many years of contemplating different ideas, the one ingenious concept I could never get out of my head and to this day I believe would be a phenomenal tribute to the greatest generation. An idea that would require a huge commitment from the American people and our government, would be to build a satellite large enough to see by the naked eye from earth that will blink red, white, and blue and glow over earth every night, including a special time each night over America for all mankind on earth to view. Also, **mandatory, at least one** year, say at the fifth-grade level, beginning on December 7 (Pearl Harbor day) and into each new year in every school in America: teaching, talking, discussing, and explaining the significance of the satellite and the greatest generation, heavily emphasizing the Great Depression and World

War II. Never to be forgotten what this special generation contributed to American's future, its culture, and making America the greatest country in history! I have even thought of some names for this satellite: "Integrity," "Indore," "Ike," and "The General," just to name a few patriotic names.

Well, you think I have appreciation and respect for the greatest generation? Hell yeah! I only wish and hope all American feel the same as I do, and if so, together we get some type of monument built in memory of these great folks. A monument that would last forever to show our appreciation. More importantly our grandchildren's grandchildren to learn and respect that generations commitment and sacrifice to flag and country, making America the greatest country in history. If I had the ability to have just one wish, I too would graciously sacrifice, with pleasure, a year of tomorrow for all future Americans to experience one year of my yesterday, a year of Camelot.

50th Wedding Anniversary
From Top Left Down: Me, Drew, Duke, Roger
From Top Right Down: Dave, Steve, Paul, Marion, Liz

Mom and Dad representing elegance